DEATH AS
METAMORPHOSIS
OF LIFE

RUDOLF STEINER (1913)

DEATH AS
METAMORPHOSIS
OF LIFE

Seven Lectures Held in Various Cities
November 29, 1917 – October 16, 1918

TRANSLATED BY SABINE SEILER

INTRODUCTION BY CHRISTOPHER BAMFORD

RUDOLF STEINER

SteinerBooks

CW 182

SteinerBooks
Anthroposophic Press

610 Main Street
Great Barrington, Massachusetts 01230
www.steinerbooks.org

Original translation from the German by Sabine Seiler

This book is volume 182 in the Collected Works (CW) of Rudolf Steiner, published by SteinerBooks, 2008. It is a translation of the German *Der Tod als Lebenswandlung* published by Rudolf Steiner Verlag, Dornach, Switzerland, 1996.

Library of Congress Cataloging-in-Publication Data

Steiner, Rudolf, 1861-1925.
  [Tod als Lebenswandlung. English]
  Death as metamorphosis of life : seven lectures held in various cities November 29, 1917-October 16, 1918 / Rudolf Steiner ; translated by Sabine Seiler ; introduction by Christopher Bamford.
      p. cm. — (The collected works of Rudolf Steiner ; CW 182)
  Includes bibliographical references and index.
  ISBN 978-0-88010-607-8
  1. Anthroposophy. 2. Death. 3. Dead. I. Title.
  BP595.S894T6313 2008
  299'.935--dc22

                    2008004395

Printed in the United States

CONTENTS

The negation of destiny resulting from one-sidedness. Intellect destroys instinctive capacity. Instinct must be spiritualized. Perception of the spirit by "bringing about another tempo." A school should give impulses for the whole of life. "The world's schoolmaster" Woodrow Wilson.

4.

Signs of the Times: East, West, and Central Europe

ULM, APRIL 30, 1918

Origin of the word "God." Earth body, earth soul, physical culture, spiritual culture. The churches. What is it that is commonly venerated as "God"? The East and the new Spirituality. Leninism as the bitterest irony. Tagore, the task of Central Europe between the Orient and Anglo-Americanism.

5.

Rebellion Against the Spirit

HAMBURG, JUNE 30, 1918

Relationships between the living and the dead. Falling asleep and waking up. The dead as counselors of the living. Lloyd George, Matthias Erzberger, Goethe's development. Faust and Wagner. Mephisto, Lucifer, and Ahriman. Psychoanalysis. Otto Weininger. Max Dessoir. Oscar Hertwig. Gibbon. Treitschke. The trials of gifted people.

6.

What Does the Angel Do in Our Astral Body?

ZURICH, OCTOBER 9, 1918

The working of the hierarchies in the human being. The aims of humanity in the future: fellowship, freedom of religion, insight into the spiritual nature of the world. The counter actions of Lucifer and Ahriman: sexual instincts, egotistic motives influencing health and illness. Misuse of technology.

7.

How Can I Find Christ?

ZURICH, OCTOBER 16, 1918

The disease of atheism, denial of Christ's misery, denial of spiritual idiocy. The Mystery of Golgotha and science. Harnack. The situation of humanity at the time of the Mystery of Golgotha. The year 333. The origin of the gospels through atavistic clairvoyance. Tertullian. The year 666. Justinian. The academy of Gondishapur. Mohammed. The Council of Constantinople of 869. Angelus Silesius. Johannes Mueller. Speech as gesture. Woodrow Wilson and Herman Grimm.

pages 127–150

INTRODUCTION

CHRISTOPHER BAMFORD

Rudolf Steiner gave over six thousand lectures. Many of these were cycles or lecture courses in which he focused on a specific theme of his spiritual research. At the same time, he also gave many individual lectures. These, like the cycles, were of two kinds. They were either public lectures or were given for members of the Theosophical-Anthroposophical Society. Naturally, when collected chronologically to constitute a volume in the Collected Works, the inner cohesion and narrative drive of such separate lectures, given to different audiences, varies. Sometimes, reading them, the themes and tones of the various lectures differ so much in quality and content that each seems to stand virtually on its own, and the collection does not seem to hold as a dramatic, structured whole. This is not the case with the lectures given in 1917-1918, and published here.

Death as a Metamorphosis of Life is a brilliant, exceptional collection. The lectures are intimate, existential, profound, and transformative: they address us in our soul lives—where we live, and where we strive for spiritual experience. They speak to our hearts, addressing us warmly and lovingly. In a rare way, although given almost ninety years ago, they are absolutely contemporary, seeming to speak to us today in the twenty-first century where we are.

They are extraordinary, too, in yet another way. They make clear the necessary and living bond that must unite the inner work of Anthroposophists—the day-to-day inner, spiritual work in our ordinary lives—and the outer work of Anthroposophy: the manifestation of spirit in life; that is, the tasks of service that we take on the world. Although given to Anthroposophical Society members at a historically critical moment—when Steiner was summoning all his forces to make a decisive contribution to the social and economic future of humanity—the lectures do not speak, except implicitly, of the world crisis, but of what might bring into being the positive changes Steiner envisioned: that is, the inner life. Presciently—for the real outer work would not begin for a year—Steiner understood that, if Anthroposophy or spiritual wisdom does not live and grow as a spiritual reality in the souls of those who claim to practice it, then the practical wisdom—their actions in the world as called for by the spirit of the times—will come to nothing.

Unquestionably, the times were dire. The year 1917, as is well known, was epochal in modern history: it was when the new and still reverberating geopolitical configuration first clearly revealed itself. The Great War, with its carnage, still had eighteen months to go before terminating in the catastrophe of the Treaty of Versailles. Thus the Great War—its politicking and its dead—is the perpetual, ever-present, heart-breaking context of these lectures.

Against this background, a new temptation to social upheaval suddenly, but not entirely unexpectedly, appeared from the East in the shape of the Russian revolutions of February and October. These revealed Soviet Communism as a mighty, persuasive power to be reckoned with. Almost simultaneously, as if to balance the threat, from the West the United States then entered the ongoing conflict with decisive, overwhelming consequences. Central Europe thereby found itself in a new position: uncomfortably placed between the conflicting propagandas of free-market capitalism, nationalism, and democracy on the one hand, and socialism in all its forms on the other.

While it was clear that life after the War could not continue as it had before, Central Europe (Germany and the Austro-Hungarian Empire) could find on its horizons no viable alternative—intellectual, social, or political—to what bombarded it from East and West. Not surprisingly, then, in search of a clear alternative to the right and left wing proposals already at work in popular consciousness, Count Otto Lerchenfeld, a German diplomat, turned to Rudolf Steiner for advice. Ludwig von Polzer Hoditz, a similarly highly placed Austrian (and Anthroposophist) was brought into their discussions, out of which arose the idea of the "threefolding of the social organism." According to this view, society was to be understood as consisting of three spheres—a free cultural life, a brotherly economic life, and egalitarian legal or rights life—corresponding to the threefold motto ("Liberty, Fraternity, Equality") of the French Revolution. Steiner would work on this idea until the War ended. Following the Peace, from about 1918 to 1922, he would then dedicate himself wholeheartedly, with every fiber of his being, to its implementation.

Coincidently, but not unrelatedly, 1917 was also the year that Steiner finally broke through and was able to clearly formulate the reality of the similarly "threefold" nature of the human organism. From the beginning of his spiritual and philosophical research—his search for "anthroposophy" or the wisdom of the human being— Steiner had understood that the human beings were beings of thinking, feeling, and willing. But not until 1917 was he finally able to clearly understand and communicate how these three functions related to the human organism in terms of the nervous, the rhythmic-circulatory, and the metabolic systems—an understanding, which would be further developed in, and become the basis of, Waldorf education, one of the most seminal, postwar Anthroposophical contributions to social renewal.

Clearly, then, Rudolf Steiner was able to work and to prepare for what was to come on both the inner and the outer fronts simultaneously. Thus, while working intensely with Lerchenfeld and Polzer-Hoditz on the conception of the "threefold social organism" as a promising model for Germany's postwar social future—and engaging in complex political maneuvers on its behalf—he was also able to write one of his most important books, *The Riddle of the Soul* (CW 21), the sixth appendix of which contains a short, schematic account of the idea of the threefold human organism. 1917 also saw the writing of his commentary on *The Chemical Wedding of Christian Rosenkreutz* for Alexander von Bernus, as well as a number of lectures, especially on topics having to do with the spiritual scientific approach to cultural topics, such as "Anthroposophy and the Academic Sciences" and "Anthroposophy and the Natural Sciences."

1918 continued the work of preparing for the end of the war, which essentially came on March 3, with the signing of the Peace Treaty of Brest-Litovsk, signaling the end of armed conflict. In response, Steiner oversaw the republication of revised editions of an astonishing number of his books, including: *The Philosophy of Freedom* (much revised); *Goethe's Worldview* (also rewritten in important parts); *How to Know Higher Worlds* (with only minor changes); *A Way of Self-Knowledge* and *The Threshold of the Spiritual* (both with new Afterwords); and *The Riddles of Philosophy* (with a new introduction).

Clearly, he was preparing to present Anthroposophy anew to the brave new world following the War. At the same time, of course, work continued on the building of the Goetheanum and the development of its artistic mission; and lectures continued to be given, especially again on themes of current public interest, such as the historical situation of Central Europe and the rise of psychoanalysis. And the work with Lerchenfeld and Poltzer-Hoditz continued to take up a huge amount of attention and time.

Little of these matters appear in *Death as a Metamorphosis of Life*, except between the lines. The rationale is clear. Anthroposophists must now prepare inwardly to carry out what will be demanded of them. As he says in the first paragraph of the opening lecture:

Just as I believe that our difficult times demand that in our public anthroposophical lectures certain things must now be said, things people really need to hear now, so I am also convinced that the time has come for us to talk among ourselves about certain truths of spiritual science.

Why? As he explains in the opening of the following lecture:

In our reflections on spiritual science we come across much we apparently cannot directly apply in our daily life, much that is seemingly far removed from our everyday life. *In reality, however, what we learn about the mysteries of the spiritual world is always, in every hour and every moment, deeply significant for our soul. What seems to us far removed from our personal concerns is at times very close to what our soul in its innermost core needs.* As far as the physical-sensory world is concerned, it's important that we become familiar with it and know what it contains. *Where the spiritual world is concerned, what matters primarily is to think through carefully for ourselves all the thoughts and imaginations that world offers us.* When we do this, these thoughts work in our soul, often without our being conscious of this. *What our soul is working on in this process may seemingly be irrelevant for us, but in reality it can be very important and exactly what is needed for the higher spheres of our soul.* (italics added)

As he says several times over the course these lectures, while books of spiritual exercises, such as *How to Know Higher Worlds*, certainly lay down the path to the experience of spiritual reality, so that anyone walking it consistently and earnestly will achieve what they strive for, there is another way to the spirit. Simply stated, it is to take seriously and thoroughly, and inwardly—meditatively—understand and make our own the accounts of spiritual realities given by the spiritual researcher. Having in this way allowed our inner life to be permeated by these realities, so that they work invisibly within us, we are transformed and can act out of our understanding so as to have the same experiences ourselves.

But where should one start, given the vast range of spiritual science? The particular realities—experiences—that Steiner focuses on in these lectures are primarily twofold and intimate: working with the dead and coming to know the Christ. What these two themes have in common is that, paradoxically, they are both earth-centered. They teach us the fundamental importance of everyday human destiny and earthly life, not just for humanity, but also for divinity and the cosmos.

Steiner begins with those in the world of the dead, who, because their lives are spiritual, not physical, can teach us much about how to live as spiritual beings on earth.

Our world is sensory. It is physical. It is in a sense a mineralized world. We see things as outside us, as objective. Therefore, we believe rocks and plants are insensate. Acting on the things of the world, we do not feel we are causing them pain or pleasure, joy or sorrow. But in the first realm of the dead, the realm of sympathy and antipathy —for just as we live in three realms (mineral, plant, and animal) the dead too inhabit three realms—even the smallest action causes pleasure or pain.

All activities there are therefore guided by the awareness that every act calls forth a living, feeling response. Everything is sentient. Our every act can cause either pleasure or pain. That is to say, the world of the dead is very connected to the animal or feeling world: it works into it and must transform its impulses.

The second realm of the dead is one of surging and ebbing will. We share this life with them when we are in dream state, which occurs not only while we sleep but continues unconsciously through what we call our waking state. Here, unknown to us (for we sleep through it), the dead live very closely with us and below the threshold of our waking consciousness permeate us with feelings, passions, and thoughts. This realm is also a "karmic" realm: it is those with whom we were connected on earth who remain connected with us. Such "karmic" links also extended to those connected with those with whom we are connected, and continue on through them to create a vast karmic community, in which we—unknown to ourselves—participate. "The circle of a dead soul's connections gradually widen" and so do ours. Thus we are linked, ultimately, with all humanity.

With the third realm of the dead, we enter the sphere of the angelic hierarchies. Through them, the dead experience themselves: that is, their "I." They experience themselves as spiritual beings in a world of spiritual beings to whom they are related, as the tenth or lowest hierarchy.

Making these ideas a reality is important on several counts. First, if we do not do so, we jeopardize our own lives after death. if we are caught too deeply in the sensory world alone, we may after death not escape its spell and remain caught in the earthly sphere. Second, if we do not understand the reality of the ways in which the dead (and the hierarchies) work into our lives, we will be failing in our responsibilities as co-workers with the spiritual world in the evolutionary transfiguration of the world. Third, and this is only implicit in Steiner, if we do not learn from the dead in these ways, we will not be able to develop capacities we will need in the future—the so-called sixth or next epoch.

Referring to this epoch, Steiner spoke often of the need to prepare the soul qualities we will need for the coming age, when each human being will feel the pain of every other human being as his or her own; each human being will recognize the absolute value of every other human being; and all human beings will feel united in the single being of humanity. As he described it, spiritual life will then be wholly individual and every human being will have his or her own religion; each of us will know complete freedom of thought; there will be no collective ideology; and reality will be universally understood to be spiritual. Working with the dead can clearly be a source of guidance in this process.

Equally important—and for the same reasons—is to understand the Mystery of Golgotha and the Christ impulse which, though historical, is completely different from any other "historical" reality, for it cannot be understood in any other way than spiritually. As Steiner says: "It is the will of the gods that the most important event on earth must compel us to spirituality." The reality of Christ is to be lived spiritually; experienced inwardly, not historically. At the same time, it must be found here on earth. Christ entered the earthly world— his kingdom is here—and here he must be found. We must enter his kingdom—place ourselves within it—then everything will be seen as essentially spiritual. One place to seek him is in human destiny: in what happens to us. The more we become aware of what is secretly, invisibly, unconsciously working in our lives, the closer we will come both to working with the dead and to the kingdom of Christ.

The second lecture recapitulates some of these themes and goes on to give wide-ranging practical advice on realizing them in our lives. He stresses, first, that interaction with the dead requires great moral discipline and purification. Our motives must be "pure and soulful," for the realm we will be entering is connected with what on earth may be called "our baser passions." He then goes on to describe how relations with the dead are the reverse of those with the living. On earth, I speak to you; but to speak to the dead is to be spoken. The words of the dead arise in our own souls. They speak with our voice. Indeed, they speak to us all the time. We are always speaking with the dead. As Steiner says, "Everyone is continuously communicating with the dead." We must realize this. We must become aware of where our thoughts, feelings, and will impulses originate. We must begin to awaken and phenomenologically attend to the source of our soul lives. The best time to do this is just before falling asleep and just before waking up.

Working with dead in such an intimate way often involves us in emotions of grief and loss, and in this regard Steiner addresses the difference between losing a child or young person and an older person. A younger person remains with us. Children who die remain directly present to their loved ones: they remain with them spiritually. We do not lose them. Older people, on the other hand, do not lose us. Though they move further away, they have the power to stay connected. A difference exists, too, in the quality of the sorrow we experience: in the case of a child, it is compassionate; in the case of an older person, it is more egotistic. When a child dies, we feel what they are feeling: we are close to them. When an old person dies, they feel what we are feeling, and we should act accordingly.

The third lecture provides yet another angle. From this point of view, the function of the study, deep understanding, and practice of spiritual science is to "set free what lives as a spiritual principle in our body, in our life story and talents, and in our destiny." We must learn to honor, nurture, and care for our spiritual individuality. Materialism, literalism, and abstraction hinder this process. We become narrow-minded, rather than expansive in our thinking and imagining. We must learn to set free our thinking and imagination. We must overcome one-sidedness, and become fluid and flexible in our souls. We must overcome linearity and learn to understand the living, flowing, rhythmic nature of cosmic harmony and inner peace. As we do so, we shall learn devotion to the spirit in all things.

The fourth and fifth lectures that follow are more general. They take the themes we have been discussing, and speak of them rather in the context of the "the signs of the times." The focus is the cultural loss of the spirit and any true understanding of the divine; and the need for, and path to, their recovery. For this, a new spiritual wisdom is needed in the form of a living Anthroposophy that begins in the cultivation of every individual's inner life. No task is more important than to find our inner life. To do so is to begin to permeate the material world with spirit, and thereby overcome the materializing tendencies of our time, whether they manifest in scientism, consumerism, or materialist economic and social thinking.

The two final lectures begin with a clarion call. Anthroposophy must not remain just a theory. It must become the purpose and inspiration for our lives and vital forces. To become real, it must become so strong and deep in us that, fulfilling itself through us, we may become "the guardians of certain specific and highly significant processes of humanity's development." Usually, one thinks that one makes one's ideas real by acting physically in the world. Certainly physical action must occur, but to happen in right way, the ideas must first become, and act, as spiritual realities. For this, we must become conscious in our "I." Such is the mission of the "consciousness soul," the development of which is the task of our epoch.

The path to such "I"-consciousness lies through coming to know the work of the hierarchies—the milieu where the "I" lives—in our soul lives. We exist only through their work; and the nature of that work changes in the course of evolution. Today, for instance, the angels, under the direction of the powers (*Exousiai*), form images in our souls or astral bodies. These images, ebbing and flowing into us, although we are mostly unaware of them, are as it were the seeds of our future soul transformation. They contain the prototypes for the kind of human beings we must become and the kind of social order we must create. In fact, it is the angels who are forming the nucleus of the above-mentioned capacities we will need in the sixth or next epoch. *First*, true community, such that no one will be happy if anyone else is unhappy. *Second*, the capacity to recognize each person we meet as bearing a divine spark within them. "We are to see in everyone a revelation from the divine ground of being, a revelation in flesh and blood." In other words, Christ is in everyone, which means that the knowledge that whoever—and whatever—we meet is a divine revelation must come to guide us in all things. From this it follows that, *thirdly*, we will become innately and individually, in our innermost sanctum, religious; and this religious sense will permeate everything we do. Meeting another human being—acting in the world—will become a free sacrament. Religious freedom—each person with his or her own religion—will therefore become the norm. In addition to all this, the angels want us to come

xviii   *   DEATH AS METAMORPHOSIS OF LIFE

to the spirit through thinking, conscious cognition. Implicit here, as Steiner says, are three profound insights that we must come to:

> The first insight is that we can understand the deeper dimensions of our nature with lively, active, human interest.... The second revelation from the world of the angels will show us irrefutably that the Christ impulse leads to religious freedom, among other things, and that the hallmark of true Christianity is that it makes absolute freedom of religion possible. The third revelation is the incontrovertible realization that the world is spiritual.

None of this will come about without conscious inner struggle and great effort. Forces in the universe—Lucifer and Ahriman and their cohorts—do not want it to happen. They will do everything they can to try to stop it. But if we truly awaken, and develop inwardly in the ways in which the dead and the hierarchies are guiding us, then, in the end, the adversarial forces may themselves see the light.

Throughout all this, as its hidden center, is the being and mystery of the Christ. And so, in the last lecture, Steiner turns to what is most important: How can one find the Christ?

He begins in Trinitarian fashion. Three fundamental human spiritual yearnings exist: to know the divine ground of the world, to know the Christ, and to know the spirit. All three are present to us; and therefore it is their lack that is puzzling. For Steiner, atheism—the denial of the divine—is basically a kind of disease, the disposition for which we all carry within us; not to find the Christ is a grave misfortune, but also a question of destiny; whereas not to recognize the spirit in oneself comes from a kind stupor, or subtly idiocy.

As for the Christ, as we know, he cannot be found by historical means. We will never find the "historical Jesus." Either we must turn to spiritual means to find the Christ, or we will not find him. The Gospel accounts, true in their own way, derive from inspired, atavistic clairvoyance; they are not accounts based on ordinary human observation and thinking. It was not until the third century or so, when the inspiration from the dead contemporaries of Jesus became available to those on earth, that a truer understanding could begin.

Here, Steiner uses the example of the Latin theologian Tertullian, who said of the Mystery of Golgotha, "It is credible precisely because it is absurd" and "He was buried, and rose again; the fact is certain, because it is impossible." Today such statements seem to make no sense, yet Tertullian knew prophetically what humanity would have to go through—what soul developments would have to occur—before Christ could be understood and encountered. The evolutionary path to that meeting point would be hard and strewn with obstacles. The adversarial powers would make an attempt to shortcut the evolutionary development, and, as a consequence, the Middle Ages and also modernity would receive a view of the human being not as a threefold being of body, soul, and spirit, but as twofold (consisting of body and soul alone). Nevertheless, people today do still bear a faint reflection of the Mystery of Golgotha within their souls and dimly seek to know the Christ.

To realize that yearning for knowledge, Steiner, obviously speaking from personal experience, cuts through directly to the point.

To find the Christ, he says, we need three experiences. First, we must strive for self-knowledge consciously, sincerely, honestly, and nakedly. However, if we truly do so, we will find that we cannot grasp what we are striving for. What we seek constantly eludes us, disappears before us as we seem to approach it. "We cannot keep up with what we are aiming at," as Steiner puts it.

Thus the second, critical experience is of our powerlessness. This powerlessness, too, is a kind of illness, which has to do with our relationship to the body; but becoming aware of it, we are already on the way to health. For, immersing ourselves in and accepting this intense feeling of powerlessness, a change occurs. Suddenly, we realize that if we let go of what we can achieve through the powers of our physical body and brain, we can give ourselves over—open ourselves—to what the spirit offers us. Then it is as though we had died and been resurrected. Out of the soul-death that is the experience of powerlessness, we become able to find our soul again, as if risen. In other words, we have a Christ experience: we feel the Savior, the healing power within us.

As Angelus Silesius wrote:

The Cross raised on Golgotha
Cannot save you from evil
If it is not also raised within you

The Cross is raised within us by the polarity of the powerlessness of our body and the resurrection of our spirit. There is no need for supersensory capacities to realize this experience: only humility and sincerity in seeking are required. Resurrection from the soul death of powerlessness is the true Christ experience that opens the soul to the presence of Christ.

Truly, these are astonishing lectures to be treasured: to be read, reread; to be thoroughly understood as something living; to be meditated and made one's own; and to be carried as a transformative gift into the world.

DEATH AS
METAMORPHOSIS
OF LIFE

1

THE THREE REALMS OF THE DEAD:
LIFE BETWEEN DEATH AND REBIRTH

BERN, NOVEMBER 29, 1917

TODAY I would like to continue with our reflections from a previous talk because they are in line with what I am convinced we must now talk about among ourselves.[†] For just as I believe that our difficult times demand that in our public anthroposophical lectures certain things must now be said, things people really need to hear now, so I also am convinced that the time has come for us to talk among ourselves about certain truths of spiritual science.

As you may remember, in that previous lecture I talked about how souls who had crossed the threshold of death are still active in life on earth. We talked then about how the impulses of the so-called dead continue to live on in what people accomplish here on earth and how the forces of the so-called dead are connected to those of the living. Today, I would like to add some reflections that are intimately connected with this topic.

First of all, the terms and images we use when speaking about this life between death and rebirth are necessarily based on our sensory, physical life here on earth and on the ideas we develop in this life; however, life in the realm of the dead is such that those terms and concepts cannot really do justice to it. Therefore, it is best to approach the life between death and rebirth from various angles. Just before the outbreak of the current war, I made an attempt along those lines in my Vienna lectures when I talked about the life between death and rebirth as it relates to the inner forces of the soul.[†] Today, I want to point out above all that what is in a sense the most important part of life for us here on earth—and, indeed, must be all-important for us—is completely absent from the experience of the souls that have passed through the portal of death.

Just think how many of our ideas and concepts come to us from the realms of minerals and plants; these include also all those ideas, impressions, and perceptions that come to us from the heavens: the starry sky above us, sun, and moon are all part of what I call the mineral realm of nature and allow us to perceive physical images as perceptions while we're alive on earth. Both the mineral realm and most of the realm of plants—but please note, I say "most of"—are absent from what souls experience in the period between death and rebirth. Indeed, what is unique and typical of the experiences of the so-called dead is that their relationship to and awareness of those two realms is very different from ours. As we have said before, it is an illusion to assume that plants and minerals feel no pain and are insensate. Our actions have an impact on minerals and also on plants, and to some extent we are right to say that this is not the kind of impact that leads to pain or pleasure, sorrow or joy. However, we know that when we quarry stones, for example, certain elemental beings do indeed experience pain or pleasure, but this fact is not part of our ordinary, everyday consciousness. That is why in our ordinary experience we can say that when we quarry stone or do anything else in the mineral realm and in most of the plant realm, we do not cause pleasure or pain to the world around us.

However, that is not what we find in the realm we enter after passing through the portal of death. There, we must realize, above all, that even the smallest thing we do—we have no choice but to use the words of our earthly language, unfortunately—even simply touching something, is connected with pleasure or pain and arouses sympathy or antipathy. In other words, in that realm of the dead you cannot even gently touch anything without arousing a sensation of pleasure or pain in what you're touching and calling forth sympathies or antipathies.

I have already indicated this briefly in my book *Theosophy*,† when I described the realm of the soul and explained that sympathy and antipathy are the most important forces of the soul in that realm; that insight has to become a living part of our thinking. As our awareness grows of how the realms of the dead and that of the so-called living work together, we must develop a sense for how to understand the way the dead handle things in their realm. And the dead are guided in all their activities by the awareness that they are evoking sympathy or antipathy, suffering or joy, that everything they do gives rise to a response of living sensation. Indeed, beyond the threshold of death there is nothing at all that we could call insensate in the sense we apply the term to our mineral and plant kingdoms.

The above describes the lowest realm we enter when we cross the threshold of death. Just as at birth on earth we enter the lowest kingdom of the physical world, namely, that of the minerals, so upon death we enter a spiritual realm of general sensitivity, where everything is capable of sensation and feeling, where sympathy and antipathy reign. This is the realm in which the dead develop their powers and are active, and that is why when thinking of the activities of the dead, we must always keep in mind that all their activities continuously send out forces bearing sensations as well as sympathies and antipathies.

What is the meaning and purpose of these sensation-bearing forces in the context of the cosmos as a whole? You see, this is an issue that only spiritual science can fully address here on earth, and you will realize how vitally important this issue is when you consider all its implications. We are living in eventful days; at the same time, people more and more insist on accepting only those explanations of the world that can be verified in the physical world, with the result that many give up in the face of current events and abandon the search for explanations entirely.

Nowadays people often give up looking for an explanation regarding the principle of development of the animals sharing the earth with us—just think of all that has recently been done to support what is known as the theory of evolution. With some justification people assume that animals have developed from undifferentiated, simple forms to more differentiated or complex ones. It would be more correct to say that animals have developed from undifferentiated creatures to ever more differentiated and complex ones, including human beings insofar as they are physical beings. By and large, the theory of evolution has entered popular awareness, and in a sense it has become part of humanity's secular religion. The traditional religions, in all their various denominations, are trying hard to accommodate and integrate the theory of evolution. At least as far as their leading representatives are concerned, these religions no longer have the courage they still had a short while ago, namely, to speak out against the theory of evolution. They have accepted it, more or less, and are coming to terms with it.

We, however, have to ask what is actually at work in the evolution of animals, in the development of more differentiated organisms from undifferentiated ones. What do we perceive in everything in the animal kingdom, not just in its evolution, but in its being, its existence? Now, people may think this strange and incredible, but what we find when we enter into the world of the dead through awakened imaginative consciousness is that what governs most of the animal kingdom are forces coming from the dead. In other words, we humans are called upon to participate in ruling the impulses working in the cosmos.

Regarding the mineral realm, what we do through our technology and machines and manufacturing in accordance with the laws of this realm is sufficient. Likewise, regarding the kingdom of the plants, what we cultivate and grow as gardeners and planters is enough. That is, in these realms we play no more than a secondary role in the time between birth and death. However, concerning the realm that is mirrored here on earth in the animals' existence, we are involved immediately upon our death when we develop powers and enter the field of forces that govern the animal kingdom—that is the region in which we are active after death. In a certain sense this is for us then just as much the basis and foundation of our activity as the mineral kingdom is now while we are living here on earth. That is the foundation on which we stand after death.

Just as here on earth the plant kingdom rests on the foundation of the mineral realm, so after death a second and different realm is supported by the first one of surging sympathies and antipathies, which continue to work in the animal kingdom here on earth. Now, in this second region the dead no longer feel only pleasure and suffering and no longer send forth only impulses triggered by sensations and feelings, which then go on working. Instead, this second realm, which rests upon the previous one, essentially works on what we could call boosting and weakening the willpower of the dead. To understand those powers of will correctly, you'll have to read the Vienna lectures I mentioned above; there I described how the human soul's willpower between death and rebirth is different from what we call willpower here in our physical life. Nevertheless, we can call it "will" even though that different will there is interlaced with feelings and another element that does not exist here on earth.

After death, this will constantly surges and then ebbs away again. In our interactions with the dead, we experience their inner life in such a way that at one moment we sense that their will impulses are strengthened and they feel stronger in themselves. However, in the next moment their will is ebbing away and practically becomes dormant. This is how the will of the dead constantly moves between ebb and flow, first becoming stronger and then weakening again. And this fluctuating movement of the will makes up a large and important part—indeed, an essential part—of the life of the dead.

However, this ebb and flow in the will not only affects the basis of the realm of the dead. It also streams into our human sphere here on earth; not into the thoughts of our ordinary consciousness, but into what we experience as impulses of willing and of feeling—I'll have more to say about this in tomorrow's public lecture.[†] After all, one of the strange things about our experience as physical human beings is that in our ordinary consciousness we're fully aware only of our sensory perceptions and our thoughts. Our waking consciousness is limited to those perceptions and thoughts; we experience our feelings as though we were dreaming them, and we pretty much sleep through and miss what is happening in our will. We are very familiar with our thoughts, but we have no idea of what happens when we simply lift our hand, that is, when our will affects our body. And while the activity of our feelings is to some extent part of our awareness—at least somewhat more so than that of the will—even what is going on with our feelings by and large still remains dark to us, much like the images we see in our dreams. Our passions and feelings—these we experience only as though in a dream; the light of our waking consciousness does not shine on them as it does on our thinking and sensory perceptions, and it does even less so on our will. Now, it is in that part of our daily life that we experience as sleep and dream that the dead share our life. That is, the dead live with souls still incarnated on earth in a physical body much as we here live with the plant world, except that we are not closely connected with the plant world but the dead have a very close connection to our feelings and passions and will impulses; that is where they go on living.

This is the second realm of the dead. As we develop and experience emotions and sensations here in our human life, the soul of the dead continues to live on in them in such a way that the fluctuating movement I described, the ebb and flow of the will—that is, the waxing and waning of the will of the dead—in a sense becomes one with what we experience here on earth as though in a dream or in sleep, namely, with our feelings and will impulses. From this you can tell how closely connected the realm of the dead is to our earthly sphere; there is really no big separation between them. As I've explained, the dead normally have nothing to do with the realms of the minerals and plants—there are exceptions, however, which I will talk about later. The dead are very active, though, in regard to the animal kingdom, which is in a sense the basis for their existence. Moreover, the dead are very much involved in the sphere of human feeling and willing, a sphere in which we are not at all separated from the dead.

In other words: after crossing the threshold of death, by experiencing the ebb and flow of the will, the dead can continue to share the life of those still incarnated in a physical body—but not of just anyone. Rather, according to a certain law, the dead can continue to live on only with persons to whom they have a karmic connection. This means that the dead do not even perceive people who are not part of their karma; such persons practically do not exist for the dead. The experience and perception of the dead is limited by the karma that they have started to build in their life here on earth. They do not even notice any living persons who are not part of this karma. However, the world of the dead includes not only the souls still incarnated here on earth but also those who have already passed through the portal of death.

Thus, this second sphere of the dead includes all karmic relationships, both the ones the person formed with those still on earth and those he or she had with souls who have already passed through the portal of death. This second sphere rests upon one that all the dead share in common: a realm of animal existence. But we should not think here of animals as we know them on earth. As I've emphasized before, the earthly animals actually reflect what exists in the spiritual world, namely, the soul of each animal's genus. That is, regarding the dead, we have to think more of the animals' spirituality, for on this shared basis I've described, there rests for each dead soul an individual karmic sphere, nothing like what we have here on earth. After all, we all enter into very different relationships in life, and no two are alike. And after death, we find in the realm of the dead only those aspects and people with whom we have entered into karmic connections.

A second law also applies to this realm: the law that reveals what this second sphere of the dead is made of and how it is organized. Initially, what works on the dead and either boosts or weakens the willpower is limited essentially to the person's most recent life on earth or perhaps even only to parts of that life. At first, the dead share very intensively only in the life of those they were very close to, but gradually they also continue to participate in the life of others they have begun karmic relationships with. Of course, this process is faster for some than for others; it varies with the individual, and the course of each person's earthly life does not tell us anything about how things will go after death. For example, we may be surprised that certain persons or souls are part of a dead person's circle of connections because we have drawn the wrong conclusions based on physical life, which is all too easy to do. Nevertheless, the basic law applies: the circle of the dead soul's connections gradually widens. The dead settle into the life within their circle much as I have described it in the above-mentioned lectures about life between death and rebirth. As I explained there, in this realm of the dead the will impulses begin to spread wider and

wider; they live within the dead soul much like our ideas and perceptions live within us during life. It is these will impulses that give the
dead their knowledge and consciousness. Generally, people are so
focused on their earthly life that it is very hard to convince them that
the dead know things primarily through their will, just as we know
things based on our perception and concepts. Naturally, this makes
communication between the living and dead more difficult.

We can say that this second realm of life after death expands more
and more. Later—but this "later" is always relative, as it happens
sooner for some than for others—the circle of connections widens
to include not only direct, immediate karmic relationships but also
the indirect, more distant ones. What I mean by this is that once a
dead soul has spent a certain amount of time in the realm between
death and rebirth, the horizon of his or her experience expands and
includes now also those souls—whether they are still on earth or have
also crossed the threshold of death—with whom the deceased had
a close and direct karmic bond. Of course, those souls in turn have
their own karmic relationships that are not necessarily also shared by
the first deceased I mentioned. In other words, person A has a karmic
bond with person B but not with person C. In the realm of the dead
we can then see person A's experience widens to include person B,
and they share life as I've described. Eventually, person B becomes
the bridge, so to speak, connecting person A to person C. That is, In
other words, A has no direct connection to C but develops an indirect
one by way of B's direct karmic connection to C.

In the process, this second realm after death grows and expands;
this is a very slow process, but ultimately this realm comprises a
very large area. In a sense, our inner experience, our inner world, is
continually being enriched by such experiences that strengthen or
weaken the will, that lead us into the life of the dead or living souls
whose realm we share once we ourselves have crossed the threshold of
death. Clearly, a large part of life between death and rebirth consists
in always making new acquaintances, if I may put it so colloquially.
Just as in this life we're always gaining experience and learning more
about the world around us, so after death we increasingly experience
the existence of other souls in such a way that we know: some things

in those souls strengthen our will while other things weaken it. This experience of our will alternately growing stronger and weaker makes up an essential part of life after death.

As you can see, this has far-reaching implications for all of life, for the existence of the whole cosmos. It shows that we are linked not just by the vague and hazy bond of unity the pantheists and mystics have been raving and dreaming about; rather, in a very real sense between death and rebirth we are forming connections, spiritual acquaintance-ships, with large numbers of people from all over the world. Clearly, then, in our experiences between death and rebirth we're not all that different and not all that far removed from people on earth, and the connection uniting the living and the dead is not just some abstrac-tion but a very real, concrete bond.

Here on earth the animal kingdom is the third kingdom resting on the lower realms of the minerals and the plants, and likewise after death we find a third realm above the two I've described. This is the sphere of certain hierarchies, of beings that never incarnate on earth but with whom we become connected between death and rebirth. Indeed, this realm of hierarchies is the one that gives our experience of our "I" between death and rebirth its vivid intensity. In the first two realms we experience "the other," but in the third realm we expe-rience ourselves through the hierarchies. And this already shows us that after death we experience ourselves as spiritual beings amidst the hierarchies, as their children, their sons and daughters. That is, we're aware of our connection to other human souls, as I have described, and we also feel ourselves to be children of the hierarchies. Here on earth, knowing ourselves and our place in the cosmos means feeling ourselves at the convergence of the external cosmic forces around us; after death we feel ourselves to be spiritual beings composed of and, if I may put it this way, organized by the joint and interdependent efforts of the various hierarchies.

Now, we usually consider ourselves the pinnacle of the kingdoms of nature—of course, this is no reason for arrogance or pride. When we pass through the portal of death, we find ourselves in the lowest of the kingdoms of hierarchies and yet as standing in the confluence of their impulses. Only these impulses emanate from above, while here on earth the stream of impulses flows toward us from below. Just as here our "I" is embedded in our physical body and is thus an extract of the rest of nature, so after death our spirituality is immersed in the hierarchies and is an extract of the hierarchies. In other words, after death we are clothed in our spirituality, much as here our body is the vestment we put on when we pass through the portal of birth.

Thanks to imaginative cognition we can get an idea of the basic organization of life between death and rebirth. And it would be very sad indeed if we could not do that; after all, where our feelings and will are concerned, we are not at all separated from the realm of the dead. What we do not see or experience firsthand in this regard is merely not accessible to our sensory perception and our thinking. We will make tremendous progress for our future development here on earth, a huge step forward for the time humanity will continue to live on this earth, once we become fully conscious of the fact that in our impulses of feeling and willing we are united with the dead. Once we have fully integrated this realization into our awareness, we will never doubt that death can rob us of nothing more than the physical perception of those who have passed away. In reality, in all our feeling and willing the dead are always present with us.

Earlier, I mentioned exceptions regarding the mineral and plant kingdoms, and they apply particularly in our era, in our time. They did not exist in earlier epochs, but we do not have to go into that now. Now, in our time a certain materialist worldview has inevitably spread everywhere, and thus people easily neglect to develop any spiritual ideas during their life on earth. As I've pointed out even in yesterday's public lecture, when people fail to develop spiritual ideas during their life on earth, they bind themselves very tightly to this earthly life as though with a spell.[†] As a result, they cannot leave it behind and, after death, become a focus for destructive forces. Many of the destructive forces at work in the earthly sphere originate from such souls caught and stuck in the earthly sphere as though by a spell. We should not judge such human souls but rather have compassion for them, for after death it is hard to feel that one must remain in a realm that is not appropriate or adequate to the dead. And in this case the kingdom these dead get stuck in is that of minerals and plants, and includes also the mineral kingdom both animals and humans bear within their bodies. Indeed, the mineral kingdom permeates all these beings.

Now, people who have not developed any spiritual ideas, after death often shy away from the life where everything they do evokes emotions and sensations. They cannot enter the realm that is at work in animal spirituality and in the human sphere, but can enter only what is of a mineral or plant nature. I can't tell you in more detail what happens there because, first, our language really has no adequate words for this, and, second, what is at the bottom of all this must be approached slowly and gradually because it appears terrifying at first sight. Still, don't think that these dead souls then completely escape the life between death and rebirth that I've described. Rather, they merely approach it with a certain shyness or timidity, with a certain trepidation, and repeatedly fall back into the realm of minerals and plants because they have chosen to develop primarily ideas and concepts that have a certain significance for that latter realm, the realm of the dead, of the physical mechanism.

As I see it, my primary mission these days is to make people aware again, with the help of such ideas and images, that the dead are working and contributing to human development. I would like to present such things even in my public talks, but I cannot do that because people generally are not willing or ready to accept such ideas. They cannot accept them largely because they have not had the benefit of what we have shared in our various branches. Nevertheless, to describe the life between death and rebirth and highlight its close connection with our earthly life is to fulfill the demands of our time, to do what is called for at the present time. For our epoch has long since discarded all old instinctive notions regarding the realm of the dead, and consequently, we must now develop new ideas. We must leave behind our abstract notions about the higher worlds and do more than just speak of spirituality in a general way. What is needed now is to realize the spirituality that is at work in the world, to realize that the dead have not simply passed away but continue to live and work with us in the historical process of human development, to realize that the spiritual forces around us are both forces of the higher hierarchies and also those of the dead. Future generations could entertain no worse illusion than the belief that the social circle and social life we develop here on earth based on our emotions and will is created without any help from the dead, and only on the basis of earthly institutions and powers. That would be utterly impossible simply because the dead are already fully involved in our feeling and willing.

The all-important question now is how we can properly develop awareness of this close connection to the spiritual world given the impulses of our modern age. After all, in the course of human evolution, our ordinary consciousness in our physical life here on earth has increasingly separated itself from the spiritual world. And to direct our earthly evolution so that we can return as physical beings to the spiritual world—that was the purpose of the Mystery of Golgotha. We must not think of the Mystery of Golgotha as a one-time unique event, the greatest event in the evolution of the earth; rather, it is still active, still at work. And we are called upon to contribute to keeping this impulse active in the right way. As I have so often emphasized, the mission of our spiritual science is deeply connected with the impulse of Golgotha; in a certain sense, the purpose of spiritual science is to help us properly understand the significance of the impulse of Golgotha for the present and the near future.

Now, you can be sure of one thing: the natural sciences, as earthly sciences that also develop into secular religions, will become ever more prevalent. Accordingly, it is utterly foolish to accuse me of being opposed and hostile to the natural sciences even in their more radical trends. Such prejudiced claims hark back to the most outdated and antiquated way of thinking. Obviously, anyone who understands the course of earthly evolution also knows without a doubt that the natural sciences cannot be refuted or disproved. On the contrary, they will continue to proliferate more and more, and the type of religious faith the natural sciences spread over the world cannot be stopped; it is unstoppable and will redound to the good of humanity. And very soon now, possibly in only a few decades, the religious denominations will no longer be able to fight or resist this trend, and the notion of pure nature, developed and cultivated by the natural sciences, will reach everyone, even the most simple and primitive people. That much is already certain.

However, something else is certain too: namely, that the more this purely scientific worldview takes hold of people's minds, the less the natural sciences themselves will be able to pursue and cultivate anything spiritual. Consequently, the spiritual must be sought by other means, albeit ones just as rigorously scientific. In other words, the natural sciences will understand one dimension of nature and life, and indeed such knowledge will be increasingly important for the tasks humanity faces in the period between birth and death. However, what can elevate us to the realm of the spirit must come from elsewhere, not from the natural sciences.

A basic and far-reaching impulse is already heralded in the way the Mystery of Golgotha has been understood up to this time, and especially so in our own epoch. Nowadays we have to acknowledge that the clergy of the various religious denominations are among the most determined enemies of a true understanding of the Christ impulse. This may sound strange, but the truth is that the way pastors and theologians present the Christ impulse is sure to alienate people from it more and more. Indeed, nowadays the denominations are further from understanding what the Christ impulse really is than ever before. I don't want to go into all the essential points concerning the Christ impulse today; after all, we've already talked about this before and will do so again. Still, I want to emphasize something that is particularly important now in regard to the Christ impulse: we must see it as completely different from any other historical impulse. Essentially, people realize this, but they still get drawn into all sorts of compromises. They settle for half measures and lack the courage to accept the whole truth. What we have to understand is that it is impossible to learn or say anything about the Christ impulse based on the usual methods of history. According to eminent theologians, it's pointless to ask whether the gospels could be authentic and true in the usual historical sense; according to them, the historical proofs of Christ's existence fill a quarto page at most.[†] That's what eminent theologians say these days. In other words, they are willing to admit that considered as historical sources, the gospels are ultimately not reliable. There is no way to prove that they represent historical facts; that's what we have to keep in mind. Even leading theologians thus admit that all the historical evidence we can gather for the gospels—like the historical documents we have about other important figures of history—will fit on a quarto page. The important point here is, however, that even what is written on that quarto page is not true in the usual historical sense.

People will have to admit that while there are historical causes and evidence for the existence of Socrates and Julius Caesar, for example, there are none for the existence of Christ Jesus on earth; his life must be understood spiritually. That is indeed the most important and essential fact about him; for regarding the Mystery of Golgotha, we will either fall into agonizing doubt if we want to rely on physical evidence—because there is none—or we will have to understand it in a spiritual way. In regard to everything else we are free to look for historical evidence, but where the Mystery of Golgotha is concerned, no historical evidence of any kind will ever be of any use to us. Instead, we are forced to approach this mystery not with our usual physical-historical methods but with spiritual understanding. If we do not want to understand the Mystery of Golgotha based on a spiritual understanding of our earthly development, we will not understand it at all. Thus, we can say that it is the will of the gods that the most important event on earth is to compel us to spirituality. We can understand the Mystery of Golgotha—which historical evidence can never prove—only if we can rise to a spiritual understanding of the world.

Accordingly, spiritual science is the only science that can speak of the reality of the Mystery of Golgotha. Everything else is outdated and antiquated, so to speak. For example, a theologian wrote a remarkable book in which he compiles all theories about Jesus of the modern age, from Lessing to Wrede, and in the process he proves that we really must overcome history as we know it and move to a new way of understanding this matter.[†] And this new understanding can be found only by way of spiritual science. Let us fully understand this, my dear friends, because the time has now come when people can experience the continuing effect of the Mystery of Golgotha only in a spiritual way. That is why I spoke of Christ's spiritual-etheric reappearance in the twentieth century and have represented it in my first mystery drama.[†] However, that reappearance will be a spiritual experience, a spiritual-clairvoyant experience.

As you can see, the Mystery of Golgotha is intimately connected with the necessary elevation of humankind to spirituality that is to begin in our time. And as we begin to move up to a certain level of spirituality, we must also realize that we can understand the Mystery of Golgotha only spiritually, in a spiritual way. In other words, the Christian faith must now be continued spiritually and not historically; it needs spiritual understanding, not historical research or tradition. But don't take what I've said merely in the abstract sense and believe that you've already done all that's necessary just because you have compiled a few common concepts and notions about the significance of the Mystery of Golgotha. Instead, it is essential that you approach this subject concretely—it is not a matter of forming ideas about Christ's life and work but rather of finding the kingdom of Christ here in our earthly sphere. After all, Christ entered this earthly world, and we must be able to find his kingdom here.

As the natural sciences gradually perfect themselves, they will show us a picture of the world that would not have been any different if the Mystery of Golgotha had never happened. In the course of earth's development the natural sciences will never reach the point where, based on the premises of physics or biology, for example, scientists will accept the Mystery of Golgotha. Instead, all sciences concerning themselves with what is happening in our world between birth and death will eventually become more and more like the natural sciences. Thus, we need spiritual science so we can draw upon the spiritual realm. The question now is how we can have not just a science of the spirit, but a way to be really immersed in the spiritual realm so that our questioning and seeking will not always lead us back to earthly nature. For we will never find the Christ impulse in nature. So how can we go beyond knowing about the spiritual realm to actually placing ourselves within it?

As you can tell from what I've said so far, we will need a certain consciousness; one that is different from our merely natural awareness, our awareness of natural facts, and is added to it. Developing this different consciousness will become increasingly important as more and more people adopt the mindset of the natural sciences as their own. For this other consciousness, grasping the Mystery of Golgotha as a spiritual fact will be the pinnacle of achievement, and this necessary spiritual understanding of the Mystery of Golgotha will then have to be extended to all of life; everything will have to be seen as essentially spiritual. In other words, we must add a new way of seeing things to our approach focused purely on the natural world.

This new way of seeing things, which must inevitably develop, will arise as we look at our destiny in the world, on both a large and small scale, with as much focused awareness as we employ when perceiving the physical world around us with our senses. What I mean by this is that now most people pay hardly any attention to the course of their destiny. But to realize how important that is, just look at some very unusual cases. Let me tell you about one such case to illustrate what I mean; this is just one case of thousands like it. Indeed, I could tell you about thousands and thousands of similar cases. For example, a man goes out for a walk on a familiar path, a path that takes him up a hill to a rocky plateau from where he has a beautiful view. He has often come here before to enjoy the view; we could say this walk has become a habit. Now, one day as he is walking along on this path, out of the blue the thought comes to him: Careful! Look out! In his mind—not in a hallucination, but in his mind, inwardly—he hears a voice asking: why do you walk on this path? Just once, could you not consider your own enjoyment paramount? That is what he hears in his mind, and it makes him think. Deep in thought he steps a bit to the side. And at precisely that moment a huge boulder comes crash-ing down and lands where he would have been standing if he had not stepped aside. The boulder would surely have struck him dead.

Now, please think about what happened there as far as destiny is concerned. And something happened, didn't it? The man does not die but goes on living. Many people's lives are connected with his, and all those lives would have changed if the boulder had crushed this man. So, something has come to pass there, but if you try to explain what happened there on the basis of natural laws, you will inevitably miss what is fateful in this incident. Of course, with the help of natural laws you can explain why the boulder came loose and why it would have struck the person dead, and so on and so forth. But whatever insights you can arrive at in this way will not tell you anything about destiny; they have nothing to do with destiny.

Now this is an extreme case, but, my dear friends, our whole life is made up of such things insofar as it is destiny. Alas, we usually don't pay attention to it; most people indeed don't pay as much attention to these things as they do to what their senses offer them as facts. Every day, every hour, every moment things happen of which I've just now told you an unusual example. Just think, for example, of how often you're getting ready to go out but are delayed by something or other, perhaps for half an hour or so. And we really have to look at these things, even at the seemingly most banal and insignificant, that happen thousands of times in our lives. In our example, you only see what happens because you have been delayed for half an hour; usually you don't think of what would have been different if you had been able to leave half an hour earlier. This is how a completely different realm continuously works on our lives, namely, the realm of destiny.

Most of us don't notice this realm and its effects because we're focusing exclusively on what is happening in our lives right now, what is under our noses, so to speak. We don't consider what is continuously being kept out of our lives, what we are spared. For all you know, you could have done something, say, three hours ago, that would ultimately have kept you from sitting here in this room now, something that might even have cost you your life—but it was kept out of your life, and you were spared. And that is why you can be here now, but all you see is what did happen and thus has already required numerous spiritual impulses in order to come to pass at all. Usually, most of us don't think about what we do in our life as the result of spiritual impulses cooperating with us. However, once we become aware of this and realize that there is a realm of destiny just as real as the natural world around us, we will find this sphere of destiny just as rich and varied as nature, but we can only perceive it clearly and plainly in special moments—in unusual cases, such as the one I told you about.

This realm of destiny, in the feelings and will impulses interwoven with our destiny, is where the impulses of the dead are at work.

Saying this will still get us labeled as superstitious fools by the "leading lights" of the day. Nevertheless, it is true that we can say with as much certainty and precision as if we were pronouncing a natural law that a voice spoke to the man I mentioned and that this was the voice of this or that dead soul who spoke to him at the behest of some hierarchies. This is how the impulses of the dead and of the hierarchies are continuously at work in us, weaving our destiny, from morning to night and especially from night until morning during our sleep.

Now, I want to draw your attention particularly to the issue of the Socratic daimon.[†] As you probably already know, Socrates, the Greek sage, explained that in everything he did, he acted under the influence of a daimon. I have discussed this Socratic daimon in my small book *The Spiritual Guidance of the Individual and Humanity*.[†] The second chapter of my recent book *Riddles of the Soul* deals with the learned and scholarly fellow Max Dessoir[†] and shows how Dessoir treats that topic, and I've spoken there also about the daimon of Socrates.[†] Basically, Socrates was aware of something that has been at work in all people even though most have generally not noticed it. Up to the time of the Mystery of Golgotha certain beings controlled the activity of the dead in human life. At the time of the Mystery of Golgotha these beings lost their power and the Christ impulse took their place. That is why there is a connection, revealed by spiritual science, between the Christ impulse and human destiny. The forces and impulses of the dead are at work in our feelings and will as I have described it; at the same time, the dead also experience alternately a strengthening and weakening of their will. The sphere of their activity is an earthly realm, just as much as nature is; and since the time of the Mystery of Golgotha the impulse living in it is that of Christ. That is, Christ is the guiding force in this realm I've described.

Consequently, in the future we need not only a proper spiritual-scientific understanding of the Mystery of Golgotha, but we also need to realize that both the world of natural facts and its opposite pole, the realm of destiny, permeate our lives. So far, people have rarely paid any attention to this realm of destiny, but eventually we must become as aware of it as we are of the natural world, and then we will realize that we are connected with the dead in this realm of destiny, which also contains within it the kingdom of Christ. In the Mystery of Golgotha, Christ descended to earth to be active here, to share with us what we have in common with the dead as long as they are still working in our earthly sphere—and here I'm talking about what normally happens, not any exceptional case.

Now, we should not take this as just an abstract truth, as a mere concept, or as a commonplace to be trotted out occasionally when we vaguely remember that it is true. Rather, thanks to this knowledge, we should feel as much at home and as much aware of everything in this sphere of destiny as we are in the natural world around us. Once we feel ourselves as much part of that sphere as we are of the world we see with our physical eyes, and thus become aware of the working together of the forces of Christ and of the dead, we can truly, concretely, and sensitively live with the dead. This is what we can then finally develop, my dear friends, and then as we experience or do this or that, we will realize that we are untied in it with our dear departed. This will enrich our lives immeasurably.

Although we say we remember the dead, we do not have a truly intense life or connection with them. Such an intense life, one that will be a true and real life because we are no longer sleeping through it and through our destiny, will only be possible once we go beyond remembering the dead to really knowing that when we do this or that, when we are successful in our endeavors, it is because the dead have been working with us. You see, the bonds uniting us with the dead are not dissolved but remain, and in the future will tremendously enrich our life on earth. The fifth post-Atlantean epoch, which is the one we're currently living in, is devoted primarily to educating humanity in the direction I've outlined just now. In fact, humanity will not be able to survive the sixth post-Atlantean epoch unless we all learn to feel these things in the right way and to integrate the reality of destiny into our awareness in the same way we now perceive the reality of the natural world.

What I wanted to emphasize today is that we must realize the connection between the Mystery of Golgotha and the problem of death in concrete terms because this is also intimately connected with what all people must now become aware of. So far, among many other things, we have lost the ability to experience true realities in our impulses of feeling and willing and have instead allowed ourselves to be lulled by the greatest illusion of all, namely, the belief that we can shape life on earth on the basis of earthly laws. We see the extreme expression of this illusion in pure materialistic socialism, which will of course never accept that the dead play a role in even the smallest of our human actions. Instead, it insists on seeing everything as determined by the laws of economics and physics. But that is only one extreme form; there is another opposite extreme, the one all sorts of idealists are now dreaming of. In utter disregard of spiritual aspects, their utopian dream is to create purely programmatic, international organizations worldwide, supposedly to eliminate war once and for all. Of course, once people have fallen for this illusion, they will soon realize that rather than eliminating war, it will actually bring about the very thing it was intended to do away with. True, there is much good will and sincerity involved here, and such utopian dreams are an inevitable outgrowth of the of the materialist spirit of our age; in a sense they are its extreme political expression and will ultimately bring about the very conditions they intend to abolish.

What we need instead is for an understanding of the workings of destiny to spread over the whole world and also take hold of legislatures and political organizations forming the basic structures of our social conditions. In fact, everything that does not go along with the necessary spiritual development of humanity I've outlined here will simply dissolve; it will decline and deteriorate. That is why it is extremely important to properly understand the signs of our times. To put it bluntly, we don't have to make politics here and will not do that; nevertheless, if we want to focus on humanity's spiritual development, we must see clearly what our epoch demands of us. In particular, we must understand that the paths most of us follow these days will lead only to losing Christ, not to finding him. We can find Christ, the only true king and lord of the earth, only by raising ourselves to spirituality.

You can be sure that these days the various religious denominations are seeking Christ in vain; among other things, they have entered into some rather strange compromises in their view of Christ to the point, here and there, of even worshipping him as a god of war. But you can also be sure that we can find Christ if we seek him where he can be found in his reality, namely, by understanding the realm of destiny as a reality. Then an international organization will be created, and as a result true Christianity will be spread all over the globe.

Of course, you know that we've not come close to reaching this goal yet. Think of all the people who want to establish world peace—and who doesn't?—and who have developed this or that program for that purpose; what would they say if you offered a program of making Christ accessible to all of humanity as a way to bring about lasting peace, insofar as that can be achieved at all here on earth? Imagine what the various associations based on "good will" would say if you were to present such a proposal to them! As we know, even the pope, the Vicar of Christ on earth, has offered a program for peace, but you will not read much about Christ in that program![†]

These issues are not taken seriously nowadays, and that is why people cannot find a path to salvation. We must understand the Mystery of Golgotha in spiritual terms, but it is also crucial that we correctly read the signs of the times and then see spiritual science as indispensable for shaping our social future. I will have to talk about these things even in tomorrow's public lecture, but in somewhat different terms. This is what I wanted to add to the earlier reflections regarding our life with the dead.

Before closing I'd like to repeat a comment of mine even though it is highly distasteful to me to have to do so. I have mentioned this before in other branches of our society, and most of you, my dear friends, already know this. However, for the sake of completeness I need to repeat it here. I don't know if you have heard some of the utterly incredible and slanderous things said about our society—things so nasty that one can only wonder about the minds thinking them up.[†] Of course, we must protect spiritual science from such vicious, nasty slander, for that's what this really is. That is why we will have to suspend our usual private talks for some time while at the same time continuing to do everything we can in support of the spiritual development our friends seek. This has become necessary because the slanderous comments I mentioned have been compiled from precisely such private talks. Therefore, I have to ask you, my dear friends, to please understand that for the time being no such private talks can take place. However, it would be telling only half the story if we said only that much; I must also add that those who want to—of course, only those who want to!—are free to talk about absolutely everything that has ever been said or has ever happened in those private meetings. In our spiritual movement we have nothing to hide as long as people are telling the truth. I've been compelled to take these steps for the protection of our society, whether I want to or not. Please bear with me and be patient; we will find other ways and means to make sure that everyone receives due spiritual attention. But first and foremost, spiritual science must not be hindered by such things that essentially have nothing to do with it. That is why I am asking especially our long-time loyal and honest members to please understand that our usual private talks will have to be suspended for now and that I therefore release everyone from any promises made in this connection.

As far as I'm concerned, those who want to—of course, they don't have to—can share whatever they wish with anybody, for there is nothing here that must be kept secret as long as it is presented truthfully and honestly. To make sure of that we must adopt the above two provisions. I am very sorry to have to make this announcement, but I know that especially those of our friends who are closest to our movement will realize that this is necessary, and will understand.

Above all, we must realize how serious our situation is; that is why a meeting such as this one is always a special and particularly solemn occasion for me. Especially now, in the midst of the current catastrophe, I want us to be thoroughly steeped in the understanding of how essential it is that we stick together in the sense of our anthroposophical motto of being linked together in spirit. Even though we will have to be physically apart for a time now, we will remain connected in spirit. This is the best farewell wish I can offer you at the end of our time together here today; perhaps for some time to come, we will be together only in spirit.

2

DEATH AS METAMORPHOSIS OF LIFE

NUREMBERG, FEBRUARY 10, 1918

In our reflections on spiritual science we come across much we apparently cannot directly apply in our daily life, much that is seemingly far removed from our everyday life. In reality, however, what we learn about the mysteries of the spiritual world is always, in every hour and every moment, deeply significant for our soul. What seems to us far removed from our personal concerns is at times very close to what our soul in its innermost core needs. As far as the physical-sensory world is concerned, it's important that we become familiar with it and know what it contains. Where the spiritual world is concerned, what matters primarily is to think through carefully for ourselves all the thoughts and imaginations that this world offers us. When we do this, these thoughts work in our soul, often without our being conscious of it. What our soul is working on in this process may seem to be irrelevant for us, but in reality it can be very important and exactly what is needed for the higher spheres of our soul.

So, today, let us reflect on what we have talked about before from various perspectives, and let's look at it from yet another angle. That is, we will talk about what seems so far removed from our physical life, namely, the life between death and rebirth. In particular, now that we've prepared ourselves to understand these matters in the right way, I would like to tell you in plain and simple terms about some things as they are revealed in spiritual science. We can understand these things if we think them through again and again; they make themselves clear to our soul by themselves. If we do not understand them, we can be sure that it is because we have not yet thought them through often enough. To explore these issues we need spiritual science, but to understand them we have to repeatedly sift through them in our soul, and in this process they will draw strength from the events life brings to us. In fact, if we look more closely at life, we will see how those thoughts are solidified by what happens in our life.

First, I would like to say again what is also clear from many of our other lectures and treatises, namely, that one of the difficulties in talking about life between death and rebirth is that life after death is completely and absolutely different from what we can imagine here based on our physical organs. Thus, to learn about life after death we have to become familiar with very, very different concepts and ideas than what we are used to. For example, in dealing with the physical world we know that for only very few of the beings around us can we say that as we carry out our will, we cause them pleasure or pain. This is true for the animal and human kingdom here in our physical world. In contrast, we are fully convinced that the mineral realm— including everything in the air and in water and also, for the most part, the plant kingdom—are insensible to what we call pleasure and pain in response to our actions. True, this not how things are when seen from a spiritual perspective, but we can disregard that for now; based on the physical world's perspective, our conviction that minerals and plants do not feel seems justified.

The world in which the so-called dead find themselves is very different in this regard, and there everything the dead do causes either pleasure or suffering. The dead cannot do anything, not even lift a finger, without giving pleasure or pain to everything around them. We must thoroughly understand this and immerse ourselves in the realization that in the life between death and rebirth everything prompts an echo; in that realm we cannot do anything without eliciting a response of pleasure or pain from everything around us. In the life after death there is nothing corresponding to the mineral or plant kingdoms as we know them here. Rather, as you know from my book

Theosophy, these kingdoms exist in a very different form in the realm of the dead; in the spiritual world they are no longer insensate.†

The first earthly kingdom that is significant, because it can be compared with what the dead encounter in their world, is that of the animals—not the individual animals as we know them, but the realm of the dead works much like the animal kingdom does here. The whole environment of the dead responds with pleasure or pain to everything the dead are doing. While here on earth the mineral kingdom serves as the foundation on which we stand, an environment we can call "animal-like" provides such a foundation for the dead. This means that from the outset the dead are living two planes higher than we do. Life between death and rebirth consists primarily of getting to know this animal kingdom, but not in the way we come to know the realm of animals here. On earth we know animals really only from the outside, but after death we come to know the world of animals *as such,* ever more deeply and intimately. This is important because in the time between death and rebirth we must prepare all those forces emanating from the cosmos that structure our body. During our life here on earth we know nothing of these forces and their work, but after death we find out how the cosmos shapes our body down to its smallest parts. In a sense, then, we ourselves prepare and build our physical body as the *summa summarum* of animal life.

To really understand this we must accept a concept, an idea, most people these days don't want to think about. For example, everyone understands that a compass needle at north-south—one end pointing north and the other south—is not acting on its own but in response to the earth as a whole being a cosmic magnet, one end of which points south and the other north. It would be foolish to claim that powers inherent in the needle itself cause it to point in a certain direction. Yet, regarding the seeds now developing in animals and humans, science and philosophy deny any cosmic influence. In other words, the very thing that would be considered utterly foolish if claimed for the compass needle is accepted as true for the development of the egg inside a hen, for example. In reality, the whole cosmos is involved in the development of that egg, and what happens here on earth merely serves to set the process in motion; but the cosmic forces imprint themselves on what is taking form in the egg. The hen herself—as is also the case for humans—is only the site in which the cosmos—indeed, the whole world system—is shaping the new life. We must understand this thoroughly because between death and rebirth we are working with higher beings, with beings of higher hierarchies, on this whole system of forces permeating the cosmos. In other words, between death and rebirth we are never idle but constantly at work and active spiritually.

After death the first realm we come to is that of the animals; to get to know it in the right way we have to sense the pain and suffering we are causing the beings around us when we do something wrong. Likewise, when we act in the right way we sense the pleasure and joy everything around us takes in our actions. We are making our way through this realm by giving pleasure and joy through our actions, and finally our soul will then reach a stage where it can descend to earth and live there harmoniously with the physical body. The soul could never descend into our physical body if it had not worked on that body itself.

After the animal kingdom we encounter the one that corresponds to the human sphere here on earth. Initially, our life after death does not include the mineral and plant kingdoms. Now, in the human realm the dead are in a certain way—one could say, regarding the concepts we are used to—limited in their circle of acquaintances. For between death and rebirth—beginning immediately after death or shortly thereafter—we can develop relationships only with those human souls, whether still living here on earth or having already crossed the threshold of death, with whom we have had karmic connections here on earth either in the most recent incarnation or in earlier ones. We simply pass by all other souls and don't even notice them. While we then perceive the animal world as a whole in its entirety, in the human realm we notice only those with whom we have had karmic connections here on earth; those are the souls we get to know better and better.

Now, you must not think that we will then be connected to only a small number of souls. After all, we have already passed through many incarnations, and in each we have entered into numerous karmic relationships from which our network of connections after death is made up. The only human souls not included in our circle of relationships are those with whom we have never become acquainted. This shows you how absolutely important our life on earth is for us in the cosmic context. If we did not go through life on earth, we would not be able to enter into relationships with other human souls in the spiritual world. Those karmic relationships have their beginning here on earth and then continue in the period between death and rebirth, and when you are able to look into that world, you'll see that the so-called dead gradually enter into more and more relationships based on such karmic connections begun here on earth.

As we've said, in the first kingdom the so-called dead encounter, in the animal kingdom, everything they do, even their smallest actions, will evoke a response of pleasure or pain in their surroundings. However, in the next realm, the human one, the dead are much more closely connected to others on the level of the soul and experience the others' soul intimately, as though they were part of it. That is, after death we get to know other souls so closely that we feel as if we were part of them; we know them as we know our own fingers, head, or ears here on earth, and we feel ourselves one with them. Our relationships after death are thus much closer than is possible during life on earth. Accordingly, after death we have two basic experiences in regard to other souls: we are either part of them or outside them, and this applies also to souls we already know. Meeting other souls after death always leads to feeling one with them, part of them. And souls toward which we do not feel this we don't even notice at all—much as we see something when we look at it and don't see it when we look away. Similarly, after death when we pay attention to other human souls, we are part of them, and we feel ourselves outside of souls we don't pay attention to.

What I've just explained gives you the basic outline of how souls relate to each other between death and rebirth. In their relationships with the beings of the other hierarchies—the angels, archangels, and so on—the dead are similarly either part of them or outside them, but the higher a hierarchy is, the more we feel connected to it after death and feel supported by it; we feel how powerfully it supports and upholds us. That means we feel more strongly carried by the archangels than by the angels and yet more strongly by the archai than by the archangels, and so on.

As you know, these days people think knowing and understanding the spiritual world is difficult, but they could soon overcome their difficulties if they'd learn a bit more about the mysteries of the spiritual world. This learning process really involves two things. First, we get to know the spiritual world well enough so that we become fully convinced of the eternal core within us. This unshakable conviction of the eternal core at the center of our being, a core that passes through many births and deaths, though still strange to many people, is really fairly easy to develop. Anyone patient enough to follow the path outlined in my book *How to Know Higher Worlds,* as well as in my other writings, can arrive at this sure knowledge.[†]

But that is only one aspect of learning about the spiritual world. The second one is what we can learn from direct contact with the beings of the spiritual world, in particular, with the so-called dead, and that is what I want to address today. Such direct relationships with spiritual beings are indeed possible, but they are a bit more difficult to achieve than the above-described knowledge, which is really easy to attain. In contrast, interacting with individual dead souls, while not impossible, is definitely not easy because it requires great care on the part of the one seeking such a direct relationship. To establish direct communication with the dead we must be disciplined and have ourselves firmly in hand, for there is a very important law for communicating with the spiritual world, we can formulate as follows: From the perspective of the spiritual world the very drives and impulses we here consider base are seen as expressions of a higher life. As a result, directly interacting with the so-called dead can arouse our baser instincts and drives if we are not sufficiently disciplined.

As long as we are dealing with the spiritual world in general while learning about our immortality, as long as this is how we encounter the soul-spiritual sphere, there is no possibility for anything impure to emerge. However, as soon as we are in contact with specific dead souls, there is always a relationship between the individual dead soul and our blood and nervous system, strange as that sounds. In other words, the dead live, so to speak, in the drives and instincts that are found in the blood and nervous system, and that can awaken our baser instincts. This poses a danger only for those who have not purified themselves through self-discipline.

This point must be emphasized because it is the reason why the Old Testament practically forbids any contact with the dead. That prohibition was instituted not because it was considered a sin to communicate with the dead if the contact is maintained in the right way, but for the reason I've explained just now.† Of course, we can ignore the methods of modern spiritism in this context. Essentially, it is not a sin to maintain spiritual contact with the dead, but when our thoughts in our interactions with the dead are not pure and soulful, then our baser passions can easily be incited. These passions are not fired up by the dead but by the element in which they live. After all, what we regard as belonging to the animal kingdom here is the basic element in which the dead live in the spiritual world, and when this realm of the dead spills into us, so to speak, it can easily turn and become base in us even though in the spiritual world it is actually a higher realm. It is very important to keep this in mind and it must be pointed out when we're talking about communicating with the so-called dead because it is an occult fact.

Talking about contact with the so-called dead also allows us to describe properly what the spiritual world is like. For what we experience in our contact with the dead shows clearly how different the spiritual world is from the physical one here. To begin with, I would like to tell you something that will seem irrelevant to those who have not yet fully developed their clairvoyance. But if we think about it, we will find it is very relevant because it is connected with real life. Once we have developed clairvoyance and are communicating with the dead in the right way, we will see why people generally know so little about the dead, know so little based on direct perception. Strange and even grotesque as it sounds, to communicate with the dead in the right way we must completely reverse the way we usually interact with others here on earth. For example, when you talk face-to-face with someone, *you* are the one speaking; you know that you're talking, that the words are coming out of your mouth. When the other person replies or speaks to you, you know that the words are coming from that person, out of that person's mouth. However, when we are communicating with the dead this is all completely reversed; everything is the other way around when we're communicating with the dead. That is, when we're communicating with a dead person, we hear our words coming from his or her mouth, as though the dead person were saying them. This is because the dead person inspires the words in our soul, and when he or she speaks to us, the words come out of our own soul. Clearly, this is very different from what we are used to here on earth. Here we're used to hearing the words we say come from us, but in communicating with the dead we have to get used to hearing our words coming from them and their words coming from our own soul.

Such an abstract explanation of the matter is of course easy to understand, but to really get used to this kind of reversed communication is tremendously difficult. And strange as it sounds, it is largely because we are not used to this reversal that we don't perceive the presence of the dead even though they are always there, always with us. Generally, we think that everything emerging from our soul originates with us. We don't bother to ask whether something we believe to come from within us actually came to us as an inspiration from the spiritual world around us. On the whole, we prefer to interpret everything in the context we're familiar with, namely, our physical world. If we receive something from outside, we attribute it to another person—and we could not be more wrong.

This is just one of the peculiarities of communicating with the so-called dead, and the one thing I want you to remember above all is that in the spiritual world everything is the other way around from what we are used to here on earth; we have to turn everything around. Once you realize this, you will have an important insight necessary for understanding the spiritual world, an insight that is nonetheless extremely difficult to apply concretely, in any individual case. For example, this concept of a complete reversal is also important for properly understanding the physical world, permeated as it is everywhere by the spiritual. It is because science and the popular mind lack this concept that we do not have a spiritual understanding of the physical world, and this lack is particularly obvious when people try very hard to understand the world. Sometimes one just has to disregard such futile efforts. For example, a few years ago, starting from certain Goethean ideas, I talked about the outer human physical organism to a large number of our friends at a general meeting in Berlin.† I tried to explain that to understand the physical shape of the head we must see it as a complete reversal of the rest of the body. Nobody understood what I was talking about, namely, that a bone from our arms would have to be turned inside out like a glove in order to turn into a skull bone. Granted, this is difficult to comprehend, but we cannot really know anything about anatomy unless we develop such ideas. I'm mentioning this only as an example, in passing. It may help you understand what I've told you today about communicating with the dead.

You see, what I've just explained is always going on—everyone is continuously communicating with the dead, including all of you as you're sitting here listening to me. People generally don't know about this because the communication with the dead happens in the subconscious mind. After all, our clairvoyant consciousness does not magically create something new; it only brings to our awareness what already exists in the spiritual world, namely, the fact that we are all in constant communication with the dead.

Let us take a closer look at how this communication with the dead usually happens. For example, you may want to know how you can be connected to someone who has passed away so that he or she will feel you within himself or herself. That is exactly what I was talking about earlier. How can the dead be in such close contact with us again that we can live in them? That is essentially the question we're addressing here, and we cannot answer it at all merely on the basis of the terms and concepts we are used to in the physical world. In our physical life we cultivate our ordinary awareness only during the hours between waking up and falling asleep, but for our whole being the other part of our consciousness that usually remains dull and dim in the period between falling asleep and waking up is just as important as our waking consciousness. Of course, when we are asleep, we are not actually unconscious in the strict sense of the term; rather, our consciousness is then simply so dull and dim that we do not perceive anything. Nevertheless, we have to consider the whole person, both waking and sleeping, when we're looking at our relationship to the spiritual world.

For instance, when you sum up the course of your life, you usually omit the times when your life was interrupted by sleep and describe only what happens in the hours between waking up and going to sleep again. In other words, we see our life as defined by rhythmic inter-ruptions as waking and sleeping phases alternate. But we're still here when we're asleep, and if we want to understand our whole being, we have to take into account both the waking and the sleeping states. When we're examining our communication with the spiritual world, however, we must consider yet another, a third thing in addition to waking and sleeping. This third condition is even more important for our contact with the spiritual world than the other two. What I am talking about here is waking up and falling asleep, both of which take place in only a short moment as we make the transition to being awake or asleep, respectively. Though these moments of transition are only short, they can reveal much about the spiritual world if we become sensitive to them.

About waking up, people in rural areas used to say—it's all chang-ing now but those of us older folks will remember this from our youth—that one should not right away look at the light streaming in through the window but rather first remain in the dark for a moment longer. You see, country people still knew all about communicating with the spiritual world, and they did not want to come suddenly into the bright light of day in the first moment of awakening. Instead, they wanted to compose themselves so they could retain something of the vast stream that flows through the human soul in the moment of waking up. Being exposed immediately to full daylight is disturb-ing, and it is even worse in cities where not only the light but also the street noises—the clanging of the trolley and so on—disrupt our sleep. Indeed, our whole culture is seemingly geared to disrupting our communication with the spiritual world; I'm not saying this to disparage our material cultural life, but we have to be aware of its pitfalls.

As we fall asleep, the spiritual world once again powerfully meets us, but we're soon asleep and no longer conscious of what is streaming through our soul, although there may be exceptions in certain circumstances. In any case, the moments of waking up and falling asleep are the most important for our relationships with the so-called dead and with other spiritual beings of the higher worlds. To understand what I'm going to tell you about this you will have to accept an idea that cannot really be applied to the physical world and is for that reason foreign to us, namely, the idea that what has passed in time and is over has not yet ended spiritually, is not yet over but still present. In the physical world we apply such a concept only to the dimension of space; for example, when you see a tree, then go away and come back later, you will still see the tree where it was before. It is still there. In the spiritual world the same applies to the dimension of time. That is, what we experience in one moment is gone the next as far as our physical awareness is concerned, but spiritually it has not passed away yet, and we can look back at it just as here we can look back at a tree and still find it in its place. Interestingly, Richard Wagner knew this, as we can tell from his words, "Time here becomes space."† It is one of the mysteries of the spiritual world that there we find dimensions that are absent from the physical world; for example, an event in the past is merely farther away from us. Please keep this in mind, particularly as you listen to what follows. It's important to remember that while we live here in our physical body the moment of falling asleep is completely over and past when we are waking up, but when we wake up in the spiritual world, we are only just a little bit farther away from the moment when we fell asleep.

Both when we're falling asleep and when we're waking up, we encounter the dead—as I said, we always have such encounters but are usually not aware of them. As far as our ordinary awareness is concerned, waking up and falling asleep are two essentially different moments, but for our spiritual consciousness the one is only a small distance removed from the other and not immediately adjacent. It's important to keep this in mind so you can understand what I'm going to talk about next. As I said, waking up and falling asleep are especially important moments in our contact with the dead, and in fact the dead are always present in those moments in our life. That is, every time we wake up or fall asleep we are in contact with the dead. The moment of falling asleep is especially suited for addressing the dead; thus, if we have a question for the dead, we can hold it, or anything else we want to say to the dead, in our soul until we're about to fall asleep. That is the most auspicious moment for presenting our questions and concerns to the dead, and it is easiest then, though we can, of course, also approach the dead at other times. For example, we can contact the dead by reading aloud to them, but for direct communication it is best when we present to them what we want to say at the moment of falling asleep; that's my view, at any rate.

In contrast, for what the dead have to say to us the moment of waking up is the most auspicious, and indeed every one of us, without exception, receives numerous messages from the dead in the moment of awakening—we're just not aware of them. In fact, in the unconscious realm of our soul we are continuously talking with the dead, asking them questions as we're falling asleep and telling them in the depths of our soul everything that's on our heart and mind. And when we're waking up, the dead are speaking to us, answering our questions and concerns. What we have to keep in mind here is that these are simply two different points, and that what happens consecutively on earth is in a higher sense actually taking place at one and the same time. Just as here two different locations can exist simultaneously, so in the spiritual world two moments stand next to each other, separated by only a very small distance, and one of them is more auspicious for a certain communication with the dead than the other.

You may wonder how we can support and facilitate our communication with the dead, and one thing we have to realize in this regard, my dear friends, is that we cannot properly communicate with the dead if we do it on the basis of the same motives that prompt us here to speak to the living. The dead don't hear or notice such things at all. For example, if you try to speak to the dead out of the same mood that animates your teatime conversations or chats with friends over coffee, you will find it impossible. We can ask the dead questions or tell them things only if we connect our feelings with our concepts or ideas. For example, if you want your subconscious in the evening to convey a message to someone who has passed through the portal of death, you can prepare your message during the day. Let's say you begin your preparation at noon, then when you go to bed at 10 o'clock at night, your message will reach the dead soul as you're falling asleep—and you don't have to convey it consciously; it happens in your subconscious. However, you have to present your question in a certain way, namely, not only in your thinking and imagination but also with your feelings and will. You must present your message in such a way that a warm and cordial interest develops between you. To do this you must remember times when you lovingly interacted with that person here on earth, then approach the soul of the departed one again in that same loving way. That is, we must not approach the dead abstractly but with sympathy and warmth. They can then be nurtured in our soul, and in the evening, by the time we're falling asleep, it has become, even without our conscious knowledge of it, a question to be asked of the dead.

Alternatively, you can approach the dead soul by reviving in your soul what your special interest was in that person. This is particularly helpful if you call to mind what you shared with that person in this life here and ask yourself what most interested you in him or her, what caught your interest, what drew you to that person. Remember in what moments you felt that you were glad to have that person's opinion, felt that he or she supported and encouraged you, felt glad to know that person and were deeply interested in him or her. Recalling such moments of closeness and interest and turning them toward the dead as though you wanted to speak to him or her, you can then develop and formulate your question based on pure feeling and interest in the dead person. This allows your question to be nurtured in your soul until it moves over to the dead person in the evening when you're falling asleep.

In our ordinary awareness we generally don't know much about this because very soon we're asleep, but often something of what we have conveyed to the dead remains in our dreams. As far as their content is concerned, most dreams are not true, but we often simply misinterpret most of our dreams, especially the ones about the dead.

We interpret them as messages coming to us from the dead, but they are often nothing more than what lingers of the questions and other communications we have directed toward the dead. Thus, we should not interpret our dreams as messages from the dead, but rather as something that originates in us and moves toward the dead. In other words, our dreams are simply the reverberation of our communication with the dead. If we had already reached a certain level of development, we could perceive a question or message we're conveying to the dead at the moment of falling asleep, and it would appear to us as though the dead were speaking to us, and that is why the communication's reverberation in our dreams seems to us to be a message from the dead, but it actually comes from within us. To understand this properly we have to have to grasp our clairvoyant relationship to the dead. When a dead soul seems to speak to us, what we hear is really what we've been saying to him or her; unless we've learned to make careful observations, we cannot know this.

As I said, the dead can most easily approach us when we're just waking up, and there is much, in fact, that comes to every one of us from the dead in that moment of waking up. You see, much of what we do in life is actually inspired by the dead or by beings of the higher hierarchies even though we generally assume all these things originate from our own soul. In fact, what the dead are saying to us is coming out of our own soul, and once the moment of awakening has passed and we're up and ready to start the day, we usually aren't inclined to observe carefully what arises in our soul. And if we do pay attention to these things, we're proud to take the credit for everything that emerges from our soul. However, what lives in all this is not just what comes from our soul, but also what the dead are saying to us; what they are telling us seems to arise out of our own soul, though in reality it comes from them. If people only knew what life is really like, they would be able to develop on that basis a special reverent feeling toward the spiritual world in which we and our dead live and have our being. Then everyone would know that in much of what we do, the dead are really at work within us. And in spiritual science this must not remain external, theoretical knowledge but must thoroughly permeate our inner life, our soul. In other words, we must all come to know that the spiritual world surrounds and envelops us like the air we breathe, and that the dead are always with us, though we are not able to perceive them. The dead speak to our inner being, which we usually misinterpret; if we understood our inner life correctly, we would know that it connects us with the so-called dead.

Now, the dead differ greatly among each other, depending on whether a particular soul passed through the portal of death at a relatively young age or does so in his or her later years. It makes a big difference whether children who loved us die or whether as young people we see our elders die. To characterize this difference based on our experiences with the spiritual world, we would have to say that when children die, the secret of being with them even after they have died is that when we look at the matter from a spiritual perspective, we do not lose those children; they are not lost to us but remain with us spiritually. Indeed, children who die young always remain directly present with us. In a moment we will talk about this in more detail, but for now I want to give this sentence to meditate on: children who die are not lost to us; we have not really lost them, for they remain forever with us spiritually. The opposite is true for old people dying: they do not lose us. We do not lose the children, and the older people do not lose us. This is because when older people die, they have a strong attraction to the spiritual world, and that gives them the power to work on the physical world in such a way that they can more easily approach and contact us. Unlike the souls of children who remain near us after death, the souls of the older people move further away from the physical world after death. However, they have higher powers of perception than souls who died young, and that is why they can keep hold of us. Basically, then, souls of people who died in their later years live on in the spiritual world because of their power to easily enter into earthly souls; they do not lose our earthly souls. Conversely, we do not lose the souls of those who died in childhood because they stay more or less near us in our earthly human sphere.

We can also describe all this in a slightly different way. You see, we don't always have strong and deep emotions in connection with our soul's experience here in the physical world. When someone dear to us dies, we feel grief and sorrow. Now, as I've often emphasized when dear friends in our society died, it is not the task of anthroposophical spiritual science to provide easy comfort for us in our loss or to talk us out of our sorrow. On the contrary, sorrow is appropriate at those times, and we must become strong enough to bear it rather than allowing ourselves to be talked out of it. Now, our grief is usually the same whether the person who passed away was young or older, but from a spiritual perspective there's a big difference here. We can put it like this: when children have died who were dear to us—whether our own or others we have loved—we have a certain compassionate sorrow. Children's souls actually remain near us, and because we were linked to them in loving relationships, they stay so close to us that they transfer their sorrow into our soul. As a result, we feel their grief and sorrow at the loss of their life, and their pain lessens because we bear it with them. Actually, the children who have passed away experience their feelings within us, and that's a good thing because it lessens their sorrow.

In contrast, our sorrow at the death of older people—whether of our parents or friends—is really an egotistical one. Those who die in their later years do not lose us after death and thus don't have the same feelings of grief and sorrow as those who die young. Though we may feel that we have lost those who have died in their later years, they do not lose us but hold on to us. Our grief at their death there-fore concerns only us, and it can thus be called an egotistical sorrow. We don't experience the feeling of the dead person's soul as we do in the case of children who have died; rather, at the death of older people we feel sorrow for ourselves.

Indeed, we can clearly distinguish between these two kinds of sorrow: egotistical sorrow at the death of older people, and compas-sionate sorrow at the death of younger ones. Children who have died actually live on within us, and we feel what they are feeling. This means that we truly feel deep sorrow in our soul only at the death of older people—and this is not unimportant. Indeed, here we can see that knowledge of the spiritual world is very important, for we can base our rituals around death and dying on this knowledge. At the death of children rituals that emphasize individuality, the individual element, will not be appropriate. Since children will live on near to us, it is better to choose a more general memorial ritual and to focus on the more general element in the soul of the child that continues to live within us. For example, the ceremony of a burial service is preferable in such cases to a specific, individualized funeral oration.

I'd say the two major churches, Protestant and Catholic, each offer the best rituals for the two different situations. In the Catholic Church there is usually no funeral oration but instead a burial service or funeral mass, that is, a traditional rite. It is something general and is the same for everyone, regardless of who the dead person was in life. And what remains the same for everyone is particularly good for children; thus, the more we can keep the commemoration so that it can be used for anyone, the better. However, for those who have died in their later years the individual element is much more important; in that case the best funeral ceremony is one that includes a review of the dead person's life story. The Protestant church provides for an individualized funeral oration about the deceased's life story as part of the memorial service, and this will be very important to his or her soul, while the Catholic funeral service would not be as meaningful or appropriate. The same applies for remembering the dead in general: for children it is best if we can adopt a sense of being closely connected to them; then we can try to direct our thoughts to the dead child we're remembering, and those thoughts will indeed flow toward the child's soul when we're falling asleep. These thoughts can be rather general so that they could be sent to more or less all the dead. However, to remember those who died in their later years, our thoughts must be individualized and directed to the particular person we have in mind. Those thoughts should deal with things that were important to the deceased and that we have shared with him or her. To communicate properly with souls who died in their later years we must call to mind the person's essential being, his or her nature, and revive it in our soul. In other words, we should not just remember what that person said that was meaningful to us; rather, we must bring to life within us that person's true nature as an individual, his or her significance and value for the world. Then we will be able to have the right relationship to and the right remembrance of a person who died at an older age. As you see, to develop the proper reverence we have to know how to relate to the souls of those who died young and of those who died in old age.

You can imagine what it means in our time when so many young people die every day that we can be absolutely certain that they will always be with us and are not lost to the world. I've already told you about all this from other perspectives, but spiritual things must always be considered from several vantage points. Ultimately, if we become aware of the spiritual world, we cope with the infinite sorrow of our time by calling to mind that the dead are still with us, especially those who died young. And through this connection with the dead, a vital, vibrant spiritual life can then develop—and it will come about unless materialism becomes so strong that Ahriman can extend his talons and subjugate all human powers.

As you may imagine, many people here in the physical world will reply to what I've told you today that it is too far-fetched for them and they'd rather have instructions on what to do every morning and every evening to develop a proper relationship to the spiritual world. They are misguided, for developing thoughts about the spiritual world is essential to establishing any connection to it. The dead seem to have nothing to do with our immediate life, but when we allow thoughts like those presented here to stream through our soul, when we focus our thoughts on something that is far removed from our outer daily life, we elevate our soul and nurture and strengthen it spiritually. For what leads us into the spiritual world is not what seems obvious and right at hand, but only what comes from the spiritual world in the first place. Therefore, don't hesitate to call such thoughts to mind again and again, to let them live often in your soul. Ultimately, there is nothing more important for our life, including our material life, than to be deeply and utterly certain that we live together with the spiritual world.

If this connection to the spiritual realm had not been lost to such a great extent in our epoch, we might have been spared the difficult and painful times we are going through now. At this point, only very few people understand this deeper connection, but in the future it will be widely recognized. Today people believe that once we have passed through the portal of death, our activity regarding the physical world is at an end. But no, it does not stop; on the contrary, there is a continuous, lively interaction connecting the so-called dead and the so-called living. Those who have passed through the portal of death have not ceased to be present, but our eyes can no longer see them. The dead are still with us. Our thoughts, our feelings, our impulses of will, all these are closely connected with the dead. And the words of the gospel apply particularly to those who have died: "The kingdom of God is not coming with signs to be observed; nor will they say, 'Lo, here it is!' or 'There!' for behold, the kingdom of God is in the midst of you."† Thus, we should not try to reach the dead through something external and superficial; instead, we must become fully aware that they are continuously with us. All our historical, social, and ethical life arises out of the cooperation between the so-called dead and the so-called living. We will become particularly strong in our whole being when we're steeped not only in the certainty and grounding we have in the physical world but also in realization that the dead are always in the midst of us, a realization we can develop out of the proper inner attitudes toward our dear departed. Indeed, this is part and parcel of any true knowledge of the spiritual world, which consists of various elements or aspects. To know the spiritual world in the right way, our way of thinking and speaking about it must come out of that spiritual world itself.

The statement that the dead are in our midst in itself confirms and corroborates the spiritual world, for only the spiritual world itself can evoke in us a true awareness of the fact that the dead are in our midst.

3

Humanity and the World

Heidenheim, April 29, 1918

Today, let us talk about the relationship that can develop between an individual human soul and anthroposophical spiritual science as we understand it here. Generally, people don't sufficiently realize that our soul's relationship to this spiritual science must be very different from that of any other science or any other body of knowledge relating to the human soul. Indeed, the spiritual science we're talking about here does not speak to the same part of our soul that any other science or body of knowledge addresses. Other sciences and disciplines teach us this or that; we learn something about the one or the other thing, and end up knowing more than we did before. In contrast, spiritual science does not relate to our soul by just offering information that we can add to our store of knowledge and then repeat; rather, it appeals to much deeper impulses in our soul, deeper than mere knowing or mere thinking. That is, spiritual science addresses—or at least wants to address—our inmost being, our deepest core. Coming from the spiritual world, our inmost being enters our physical human life when we are born, and at our death it returns to the spiritual world to work on other tasks. To understand the full significance of spiritual science for the human soul, we must accept in our thinking and feeling what its true relationship to the external world and to our life is.

You see, to fully understand ourselves as human beings we must realize that when we take on our physical body at birth, something lives and develops within us, something that accompanies us throughout life, from the inexperienced state of childhood through our adult years of gaining experience and becoming more skillful, through our destiny as it unfolds within us. In other words, everything that happens in our body and our life is really due to the transformation of a spirit-soul being that has lived in the spiritual-soul realm long before our birth or conception. And the spiritual science we're talking about here is addressed to this soul-spiritual being living within our body.

You may wonder why we should concern ourselves with our spirit-soul being at all since it can surely make its way in the world by itself. On the contrary—it cannot do so. Our spirit-soul being seizes us, so to speak; it permeates us and, in a sense, clothes itself partially in our physical body, our abilities, and our destiny. In fact, in the developmental phase we have now reached and which sets the direction of our future development, it is more than ever before in our interest to set free what lives as a spiritual principle in our body, in our life story and talents, and in our destiny. Ultimately, we cannot escape the spirit; it lives in us whether we pay attention to it or not. Even the most idle and easy-going people who've never made any effort to develop any religious or spiritual inclinations of their own but have remained lethargic and impassive—even they are not without spirit. To call anyone spiritless is always wrong; nobody is without spirit, and nobody can live in this world without spirit. Our spirit and soul are our innate gift given to us as we come from the spiritual world to enter this physical one, and each person's portion of this gift is based on what he or she went through before descending to their current life on earth. Thus, we are never without spirit, but we can choose to ignore the spirit within us. We can even go so far as to practically offend the spiritual within us by refusing to set it free. We may want to allow it to live in us, to cloak itself within us, but may refuse to liberate it, to set it free in us.

Once we can look at human life like this, our outlook on life will change, which is much needed indeed. As a result, when we come across impassive and insensitive people, we will not condemn them as being spiritless but will understand that they have committed the sin of burying the spirit within them during their life here. They have left their spirit under the spell that has bound it to the physical body and have allowed it to enter only their outer life and to degenerate in their destiny. We only become human beings at birth because our spirit-soul individuality comes down out of spiritual-soul worlds and enters our being. In early childhood we are as yet imperfect and unclear expressions of that spiritual individuality, which is nevertheless already present within us. We are free to ignore this spiritual individuality or to free it from the spell that bound it to our body; we can gradually release it from our body, our life story, and our destiny. Indeed, releasing it is our mission and will become an increasingly urgent task in the future—it is up to us to keep the spirit from deteriorating. While we cannot kill the spirit within us, we can let it deteriorate if we force it into a path different from the one it takes when we set it free.

Once we've made up our minds to learn something about the spiritual worlds, we draw such knowledge from within ourselves—everything else serves only as a suggestion. The knowledge itself, everything you've ever learned about the spiritual worlds and spiritual science, has come from inside you. It has lived deep inside you and had to get out; it simply had to come out. Indeed, it is destined to be brought out, and we offend against the world order if we condemn the spirit to remaining within our physical body, for there it will go astray and will be doomed to a destiny it was not supposed to have. To set the spirit free we must release it from its captivity in our physical body. As we consciously permeating ourselves with the spirit, we set free what wants to be released out of the depths of our being. It is essential that we understand this.

Indeed, we must realize that the problem with materialism is not that it simply suppresses any dissenting views or promotes the wrong view; rather, the problem is that materialism diverts what wants to enter our soul as knowledge and sensitivity, and guides it downward into coarse matter instead and lets it run riot there. Ultimately, we will have to decide in the near future whether we want to allow the spirit to proliferate unchecked in the realm of matter, or whether we want to transform the spirit into thoughts, feelings, and will impulses. If we choose the former and the spirit runs riot in matter, it will become deformed and fall into a diabolical, Ahrimanic madness. But if we choose the second option and transform the spirit within us, it will live in our midst and will complete what it set out to achieve when it entered earthly life through us. For what the spirit wants above all is that we participate fully in the life of the earth, and that is why we should not hold it back, but release it. The more we resist learning about the spirit, the more we hold it back and force it down into the realm of matter, which as a result becomes worse than it is. The spirit, too, has its assigned mission: to enter into life on earth by way of our soul development and thus to bring blessings. If it is thrown back into the realm of matter, it will work there to disastrous and devastating effect.

All these insights are results of spiritual science, and you can easily see their great relevance to our life. Spiritual science is not intended as just another theory, one among many; instead, its aim is to help us set the spirit free, to release it from its captivity in our human nature so that it can accomplish what the spiritual worlds want to achieve here. That is also the reason why many people still resolutely reject spiritual science even though they're only too willing to accept other sciences. After all, other sciences flatter people's pride and vanity and do not claim to be anything real; they only promise to give people new ideas, train their intellect, and perhaps even give them a few useful moral concepts. No other science claims to address the core of our being and to originate from worlds where the spirit has been given a mission to fulfill—only spiritual science does. Basically, spiritual science is very serious about what we need to know, and that's something people shy away from. They'd rather keep spiritual science—like everything else—comfortably burbling along on the surface of their life. People are afraid of anything directed at the core of their being, and that is one reason why they reject spiritual science.

If people were to accept spiritual science, there would be many changes where society and history are concerned, and people would have to change their thinking even in ordinary, everyday life. And those changes are what are essential—studying other sciences does not change us; we remain the same, only richer in knowledge. In contrast, we cannot study spiritual science without being changed by it, and that is how it is supposed to be. Spiritual science gradually and slowly transforms us as we study it; we must be patient with the process, but it happens unfailingly because spiritual science addresses itself to other tasks of humanity, to different elements of our human nature, than the other sciences do. Studying human nature reveals that human life is very diverse and unfolds essentially in three streams or soul impulses: imagining, feeling, and willing. These three pretty much cover everything that makes up our life, and all three have a particular relationship to the element in our soul, in the core of our being, that spiritual science calls upon.

To begin with, let's look closely at imagining. You see, the ordinary sciences and their impact on children's education, and thus on our long-term destiny and practical everyday life because it is to thoroughly shape our children's development, all this does not nurture our imagination. This prevalent development began not that long ago, maybe a few centuries ago, and by now people hardly notice it anymore. It will not be long, however, before people will become more and more aware of the things I'm talking about here. You can study scientific concepts, especially as they are now taught to our children, all your life without having to make any changes in your thinking or imagining. In fact, you not only remain unchanged, but your intellect also becomes undeniably ever more limited thanks to those scientific concepts that increasingly are a staple of public education. As a result, our thinking spirit becomes too stiff to make its way into living conditions that are much more complicated than we can know based on our ordinary knowledge alone. You see, it is heart-rending to look deeper into life, to see how people immersed in current scientific concepts are becoming less and less able to understand living social connections and the demands our society makes on us—that they are gradually pushed away from true life.

For example, as I've said here the other day and also elsewhere, if parliaments and legislatures were made up only of people who are steeped in the modern worldview, who have been educated on a natural scientific basis, we'd see that the decisions made by these learned people with their scientific thinking will reduce our social institutions to rack and ruin. Concepts and thinking based on the natural sciences can never bear fruit for our social existence. We find the same in many other areas too; in every case we lose a certain mobility and flexibility of spirit due to merely intellectual knowledge. Once we apply the concepts of spiritual science, though, everything changes. Among other things, you'll notice the state of your spirit as you try to understand what spiritual science offers, and that it differs from the one you need when learning what the outer world offers these days under the name "education." Doubtlessly, spiritual science meets with resistance because understanding it requires us to be flexible and fluid in spirit. In contrast, people find it easy and effortless to navigate the current offerings of popular and cultured literature—and they feel even more at home with its offshoot, namely, journalism, and are happy to get their education from the Sunday papers. And in lectures these days, people usually get the material in bite-size portions and are shown pictures and slides so they don't have to think for themselves at all and don't have to get their spirit moving. Clearly, none of this liberates our thinking, imagining spirit; instead, we become increasingly narrow-minded and limited, and our spirit loses its unselfconscious nature. In other words, the intellectual education now prevalent leads to spiritual narrow-mindedness.

While there has been great progress in intellectual education, especially in regard to the natural sciences, it is nevertheless a path to narrow-mindedness and limits our thinking and imagination. In contrast, to understand spiritual science we must call upon something very different in our imagination, in our mind. It is thus not surprising that people are afraid of taking even the first step toward spiritual science, and after reading just a few pages many complain that they are getting lost in the text and cannot follow it, that it is too fantastical for them. But there's nothing fantastical about spiritual science; it's rather a matter of people having lost the ability to really free their thoughts, to immerse themselves in reality with them, and being too dependent on the outer sensory world dictating and guiding their thoughts. One of the things spiritual science does for us is to call on that force within us that throws off the shackles of narrow-mindedness and frees our thinking—our mind—to understand not just a little, but very much indeed.

As I said in a public lecture in Stuttgart recently, in spiritual science we do not care whether a person is a materialist or a spiritualist; that's irrelevant.[†] And I mean this seriously: it really does not matter; what does matter is to develop sufficient spiritual strength to advance in the right way. If you have that strength, you'll find the spirit even if you are a materialist. You'll find it in matter and its processes if you're consistent in your search. And even if you are a spiritualist, you won't spend all your time chanting "spirit, spirit, spirit"; you will also be immersed in material, practical life and will work to reap the fruit of your thinking in your actions. In other words, versatility is what modern life demands—and the future will demand it even more—and versatility is the first gift spiritual science offers. Indeed, this is precisely what we need as we prepare for the future. When you look at life today and the catastrophic events all around us, you'll see that one of the deeper causes of our current catastrophe is that so many people have become one-sided. Despite advanced scientific education, they're not able to see and understand things from various angles; their spirit, their mind, is not flexible enough to immerse itself in reality. In contrast, flexibility is precisely what we gain through our involvement with spiritual science.

Spiritual science also bears fruit for our feelings, for when we think of the way spiritual science calls on us to think and get used to a much more fluid world, we are setting something free that usually lives concealed within us and allow it to unfold. In fact, the rhythm of the cosmos lives in our feeling, which we bring with us from the period before birth—it does so to a much greater extent than people usually believe. There's even numerical proof for this, but very few people know anything about these mysteries of life. Don't be scared or shy, and join me in taking a closer look at how the rhythm of the cosmos lives in our organism and all its processes. For example, we all know that the sun rises at a slightly different spot from year to year; it moves a tiny bit every year. In ancient times the vernal equinox was in the sign of Taurus, and later in Aries; it has continued to move every year, and occurs now in the sign of Pisces. In other words, the sun does not rise at the same spot in the heavens on March 21 of every year; that is why we see it circling the earth. It is only after about 25,920 years that the sun returns to the same spot, having come full circle, or seemingly so, in completing its elliptical orbit. That is, in about 25,920 years from now the sun will again rise at the exact same point in Pisces where we saw it rise today. This vast interval of 25,920 years was called a great cosmic year by the Greeks. Now, the curious thing is that to get the number of days of this cosmic year, we must divide 25,920 by 365; the result is 70 or 71. That is, one day of the great cosmic year is 70 or 71 earthly years long. Interestingly enough, that is the average human life span. In other words, taking our average life span as one day and multiplying it by 365 gives us the Platonic or cosmic year. This is the time it takes for the sun to complete its orbit once and return to its exact position: 365 cosmic days, one of which is the average duration of our earthly life.

It's a beautiful rhythm. Still, there's more to it. For example, we take about 18 breaths per minute. Multiplying these 18 breaths by 60, we get the number of breaths we take in one hour, and multiplying these by 24 tells us how often we breathe in one day and one night. Now, 18 multiplied by 60 and then multiplying the result by 24 comes to 25,920. In other words, the average number of breaths we take in a day is the same as the number of earthly years the sun takes to complete its orbit once, that is, one cosmic year. Our breath and the progression of the sun across the heavens share one and the same rhythm. On average, we breathe 25,920 times a day, and in a sense each day is like one breath because in the morning our physical body and ether body breathe in our "I" and astral body, and at night when we fall asleep, we breathe them out again. Thus, every day is really one inhalation and one exhalation. Now, let's calculate how often this happens in one solar day or the average human life span—that is, in 70 or 71 years. When we multiply the figures—you can do the math yourself—we get 25,920! That is, our daily breathing in and out occurs pretty much exactly 25,920 times over the average life span, and that is also the number of days we live through in our 71 years. Thus, each breath is to the total number of breaths in a 24-hour period as the advancing of the vernal equinox in one year is to the movement of the sun over a period of 25,920 years. Our earthly life is to the great cosmic year what one day is to our whole life, and there are as many 24-hour periods in our lifespan of 71 years as there are earthly years in the revolution of the sun back to the same spot.

Let yourself feel what this means, the grandeur of being part of the beautiful rhythm of the glorious sunlit cosmos, of our inner life expressing even in a purely mathematical way the grand cosmic music of the spheres! When we really allow ourselves to feel this, we will know ourselves as a microcosm in relation to the vast macrocosm and will realize that the great infinite world of the gods has created its image in us. This is something we can really feel and experience, and the feeling of being part of the cosmos, of participating in the spirituality of the world, is what spiritual science gives us. In contrast to our usual narrow, closed-minded focus on our "I," with this feeling we really open ourselves to the world. We are an image of the gods but don't ordinarily realize this; we only begin to feel ourselves an image of the divine world, a microcosm in the macrocosm, when we come to know ourselves through our feelings. Of course, this is a slow and gradual process. I'd like to sum it up in these words: just as we go through life by slowly living one day after another, so immersing ourselves with our feelings in spiritual science will gradually create the above-described feeling in us. And it is vitally important that we develop this feeling, for it will inspire us to undertake the great tasks the future will bring.

Even though this still sounds strange, it is nevertheless true that within the next fifty years so much will be demanded of us that unless we have developed this world-feeling within us, we will no longer be able to build factories or grow crops. Our current catastrophe is just one of the symptoms of the impasse we have reached; though the world has advanced, we've not kept pace with our thoughts and feelings. That is why they are don't enable us to really deeply under-stand this world and to live and work in it harmoniously. On the contrary, disharmony will grow among us and there will be more and more strife and warfare unless we can learn to enter into the cosmic harmony with our feelings and carry these feelings into everything we do, even into the smallest and most mundane things. Clearly, spiritual science is closely connected with what must directly intervene in our outer cultural practices if we're ever to get out of our impasse. In the future we will not be able to build factories or schools unless we can develop new concepts based on our grand cosmic tasks. These tasks have already been there for a while, but people have ignored them, and that is the cause for our current catastrophe. Indeed, the deeper causes for the catastrophe of our time can be found in what I've explained today. The divine signs that are expressed in these catastrophic events must be heeded; all of us must learn to develop a conscious relationship to the cosmos because nothing else will work.

Let me give you an example; many may still call it foolish or denounce it as mad, but it applies nonetheless. What I mean is that while great progress has been made, for instance in chemistry, it was achieved without the world-feeling I've just described. In the future we will have to add this feeling—in other words, the lab bench will have to become an altar. The service to nature we're involved in even in chemistry experiments must be permeated by the realization of the great cosmic laws that govern the lab bench at all times; for example, when we dissolve one substance in another to obtain a certain precipitate. We will approach our work quite differently and make quite different discoveries once we feel ourselves part of the whole universe. While the discoveries made up to now are doubtlessly great, they can't bear fruit for us in the right way because they were made without reverence, without the feeling of being steeped in the cosmic harmony. Over the centuries, many people have speculated abstractly about what Pythagoras meant by the music of the spheres.[†] Those speculations are clearly devoid of any feeling for the rhythm that permeates the cosmos, for the music of the spheres is experienced in that rhythm—that is what Pythagoras meant. He was not talking about something abstract but about a vivid, real feeling. What would happen if we didn't open our soul to our feelings in this way? As we've just said, for one thing, our thinking and imagining must become more fluid, versatile, and open-minded. Likewise, our feelings must become generous, receptive, and open to the world—in other words, the opposite of philistinism. And this philistinism is the very thing our modern culture—which is a great blessing, according to many materialistically thinking people—has raised from its resting place at the bottom of our soul. Nothing can vanquish this philistinism except open-mindedness and generous receptiveness of the soul, the feeling that we are a microcosm within the macrocosm, and reverence for the divine-spiritual that wafts and pulses through the world. Thus, where our mind and imagination are concerned, spiritual science must overcome intellectual narrow-mindedness, and regarding our feelings it must vanquish philistinism.

A third development concerns our will, which we're still in the beginning stages of exploring and understanding. So far, only psychologists and those who know the human soul intimately can see what is being prepared and will eventually appear. Despite what many people believe these days, those who can see deep down into the course of our development know that where our will is concerned nothing is so prevalent—now even more so than ever before—as clumsiness. It threatens to turn into a terrible evil in the future, a development whose beginnings we can already see. For example, people nowadays are instructed to do this or that one-sidedly. However, if you tried to do something but have not learned the right moves through hands-on instruction, you will not be able to figure it out. To mention a very ordinary example, if I may: many people these days could not sew buttons on their pants if they had to because they were not taught. Only very few people can do anything that's not directly related to what they have learned or been trained to do. Clearly, that is a deplorable development and must not be allowed to gain ground. For if we were to become as one-sided as our so-called blessed modern culture wants us to be, we would waste our spiritual legacy that we brought with us out of the spiritual world when we descended into this life at birth. To really understand how all these things are connected we must get beyond merely considering them theoretically and become vividly engaged in spiritual science. Then one-sidedness will be anathema to us, since spiritual science will evoke a feeling in our soul that helps us to be more fluid and versatile.

The more we study spiritual science, not just intellectually but by fully immersing ourselves in it so that it flows through our soul the way blood flows through our body, the more fluid and versatile we become in responding and adapting to the world around us. In fact, we will be able to do things we've been too clumsy to do before because we become more skilled in our willing and thus also more adaptable. You may want to object here what many people say about our Anthroposophical Society, namely, that its members don't seem to be particularly skillful or able to cope with life. Now, I'm not saying this, but merely repeating what others have said. What they're talking about is really an indication that we have not yet reached the point where the anthroposophical life has permeated our souls like blood permeates our body. Rather, the bad habit to approach everything only with the intellect or the power of reason has been carried in from the outside. For many people spiritual science, too, will just be another theory, something to think, but not something they live, not part of their being. If you only think spiritual science, then it doesn't matter whether you read a book about spiritual science or a cookbook—though perhaps the cookbook may be of more use to you. We have to take spiritual science so seriously that it really takes hold of our soul, of our whole inner essential being. Only then can it move into our limbs and loosen them up, and as a result we will become more skilled at living, better able to cope with life. To this end we must develop an inner conviction and not be satisfied with the outer one.

Once you engage in spiritual science in a lively, zestful way and realize its value for your inner life, you will find that it can prolong physical life. People may object that this or that anthrophosophist died at only forty-five or only twenty-seven years of age, but we simply have to ask in return: how long would the Anthroposophist who died at forty-five have lived if he or she had not become involved with spiritual science in his or her twenties? And regarding such matters of the inner life, the external methods of proof don't apply; statistics and the like are of no use to us here. They're very useful for outer life but do not even begin to touch on the principle of life. For example, it makes sense to base insurance policies on statistics and arithmetic, to insure individuals on the basis of calculations regarding how long they're likely to live. Still, it wouldn't occur to us that we have to die when the insurance company's actuarial calculations say we will die. In other words, we don't let calculations determine our reality; they're important and even decisive for outer life, but have no relevance for our inner life. Statistics, probability calculations, and the like are valuable for outer life, but are useless when it comes to evidence for the spiritual. You'll have such evidence when you accept spiritual science as an elixir, as an elixir of life that will enable you to fit into the larger context of life, and that will lead to many new developments.

Some time ago I was saddened at what I saw when I was eating dinner at someone's house—and perhaps, as some claim, being saddened by this makes me a strange fellow. At any rate, all during dinner my host weighed out his portions of meat and vegetables on a scale. He had to weigh out every item so as to know how much to eat. You can imagine that if we all wanted to weigh out our exact portion of rice or cabbage at every meal, chaos and uncertainty regarding our instincts would result. And we would owe this uncertainty to purely intellectual science, which can only address outer facts with its statistics and other methods. However, the point here is not that we'd be losing our instinct—and intellectual education will indeed stunt it—but that we must spiritualize it so that we develop an instinctual certainty, so to speak, in our spiritual life.

This is what I wanted to point out today in regard to our will. Spiritual science makes its way into our willing, and changes it so that we become more skilled for the world around us without even noticing how we gradually grow into what surrounds us. The closer we grow to the spirit, the more and the better we grow into the world around us. To this end, we must become able to experience the spirit, which spiritual science enables us to do. Experiencing the spirit will become increasingly important for us in the future.

After all, how do we experience what we bring with us at conception or birth? To understand this, let's use an analogy. For example, when a cannon is fired at some distance from you, you'll hear the explosion, and just before that you'll see the flash of fire. If you yourself were shot off with the cannonball and flew through the air alongside it at the same speed of sound, you wouldn't hear the sound at all. In other words, when you move at the speed of sound, you can't hear the sound at all. Similarly, we don't notice the spirit working in us because we're moving from birth to death at the same speed at which the spirit works. But the moment you begin to take in the truths of spiritual science, you move at a different pace than your body, and then you begin to see the world in a new light. In other words, just as we perceive sound only if we don't move at the speed of sound, so we notice the spirit's work in our life only if we change to a different pace by cultivating inner peace, as I've outlined in my book *How to Know Higher Worlds.* We must not live at the speed of our body but must develop a different pace—and developing this is of the utmost importance for humanity.

Nowadays people don't think or know much about what life was like in the past. History may indeed be mostly a fabrication, but that's not what I want to talk about today. My point here is that in earlier times people were raised differently, with more attention given to their feelings and disposition. The predominantly intellectual life and education we have now has only developed in the last four or five centuries, and does not take into account that we are multifaceted beings. Our intellect is indeed very malleable and capable of being developed, but only up to a certain point in life; after that it cannot be developed further. This is especially true in our current epoch, where our head, which is the seat of the intellect, is capable of further development at most until age twenty-eight. While our intellect can be developed especially while we're still young, this ends when we are about twenty-eight years old—that is, our head is capable of being developed for only about a third of our time here on earth. In contrast, the rest of our organism remains capable of further development throughout our whole life and continues to place demands on us throughout life.

These days, schools give us only what I call head knowledge, that is, purely intellectual knowledge that speaks only to our reason, and no heart knowledge, or knowledge that addresses our whole organism. Head and heart really have to be in constant interaction regarding our ethics and our soul, but nowadays this interaction is impossible because in our schools we give our children only knowledge for the head and not enough for the heart and the rest of the organism.

By age thirty-five that is a problem because then we have, at most, only what we remember of the head knowledge from our school days, and can recall that intellectually. However, we're currently not taught in school in such a way that we later are able not just to recall what we learned but can actually lovingly enter with our feelings into the learning we absorbed in our youth and have it still present within us so that we can revive it. That is the ideal spiritual science pursues where education is concerned—more than mere recollection. Of course, these days people don't even recollect what they've learned and usually forget everything once they've passed their final exams. And if we do remember, we don't usually recall our school years very fondly. In contrast, with spiritual science you can feel when you recall those years that the dawn of your life is shining into your soul, and that as a result of getting older you can now transform that recollection into something new. You'll realize then that what you learned was taught in such a way that you not only remember it but can also transform it and make it new.

Once we renew education and our whole culture with the principles of spiritual science, we will be able to breathe new life into what lives in our soul, and as a result we will see fewer symptoms of premature aging. If we study humanity's development properly, we'll see that prior to the fifteenth century even the oldest people in the population were not as old as many people nowadays already are in their youth. Symptoms of advanced aging are spreading everywhere and can only be controlled if we steep ourselves in the feeling that what we learn in our youth can then be transformed as we get older and can become new for us. In other words, what we learn is not just to be recalled later but also to be transmuted because we remember our school years fondly as heaven on earth. As an elixir of life, spiritual science will bring about this change in our daily, practical life and in our schools, and turn them into places where all of human life, our whole life span is considered. For what we give our children in their school years reemerges in a different way in their old age. For example, when we teach children in such a way that they develop admiration and reverence for something, those feelings will reappear in their mature years after remaining dormant in the intervening period. When these feelings emerge from their dormancy in our later years, they enable us to have a positive effect on children. As I've put it in a previous public lecture: if we have not learned as children to fold our hands in prayer, we cannot spread them in blessing when we are old.[†] The feeling associated with folding our hands in prayer reemerges in our old age, transformed into the capacity to bless others.

We don't even realize what we're giving our children from age seven to fourteen, as well as earlier and after age fourteen, with our modern education for their later life. This is a very serious issue because in those early years the foundation is laid for the megalomania, arrogance, and prejudice we find among our young people, and especially for the notion that they could already have a "standpoint." Nowadays even the youngest ones proclaim about this or that, "that is not my standpoint." These days everyone must have a standpoint, but it is of course impossible to have one at the early age of twenty, something people are unfortunately no longer taught.

In summary, what lives within us will once again be brought to bear upon reality, and reality will be brought into a wholesome relationship to our soul—that is the ideal spiritual science is striving toward regarding the relation of our soul to reality. Regarding the larger context of life, people often say things without any connection to reality; and if we know how our soul should relate to reality, then it's agonizing to hear them and to see the form modern thinking now takes. Children suffer such agonies unconsciously when their teachers think like that. For example, recently I attended the inaugural lecture of a renowned professor of literature, which he began by saying we could ask this or that question and listed some he planned to answer in the course of the semester. Then he exclaimed, "Gentlemen, I have led you into a forest of question marks!" I had to imagine a forest consisting of countless question marks, but people whose powers of imagining and picturing are impoverished would be facing this forest without having a picture of it in their soul. We must not underestimate the gravity of such a situation, but must continue to strive for a living relationship to reality.

Recently, a statesman said that our relationship to the neighboring monarchy is the crucial point that must guide the direction of our future political decisions. In other words, the relationship between two countries is a point and then becomes a "direction"—well, it's hardly possible to think of anything more unreal. You can probably guess that this person's soul life must be very far removed from reality to produce such cant and phrase-mongering. Of course, such a soul is just as removed from our outer social life and does not immerse itself in it. Whatever it happens to dream up will never become real. Spiritual science makes it impossible to indulge in the unreal thinking that leads to the phrase-mongering that is gaining ground nowadays. But people are so deluded and arrogant these days that they believe themselves to be especially practical, even though they have only become schoolmasterly and have really lost touch with life. Indeed, future generations will find it strange that in our time people are so impressed with the "world's schoolmaster," Woodrow Wilson, whose thinking has not even the slightest hint of a connection to reality and who is never saying anything real or true.† Still, people admire him anyway, even those who have a few scruples because their country is at war with him. Surprisingly enough, even many of the Central European powers think highly of Woodrow Wilson. Future generations will find it particularly puzzling that political programs without any relation to reality are now being developed in which the noble ideals of international understanding and world peace treaties are set forth. If only it were that easy—after all, abstract thinkers since the time of the Stoics have been dreaming of this! The ideas now hailed as Wilsonian have actually been around since the dawn of humankind, as those familiar with these ideas know very well. Of course, if we think in a healthy way, we'll have to admit that if such ideals have always been around but have never been realized, they're clearly not healthy for us. We only delight in such unreal ideas if our thinking has become estranged from reality.

All these things are connected with the most profound principles and impulses of life, and there is so much chaos and confusion all around us nowadays because so many people have adopted a way of thinking that they believe to be a match for practical life, but that is actually far removed from true reality. The ideal that spiritual science wants to bring us is the combination of reality with a resolute thinking that is strong enough to enter into reality. To attain this we have to start with our children at an early age and develop in them a sense, not for abstract concepts, but for what is real, what can be imagined. Of course, this means that we ourselves must first develop such a connection to reality. For example, if we want to teach children about immortality by showing them a butterfly emerging from its chrysalis but do not believe in immortality ourselves, we're not actually teaching the children anything. When we are engaged in spiritual science, we know that the butterfly is the true image of immortality created by the spirit of the world; we believe in this image ourselves, and for our teaching we choose only what we believe in ourselves, only what we know or strive to know. In this way we immerse ourselves in reality and work on vanquishing our egotism that wants to hold on to abstractions in our thinking. As we immerse ourselves in the spirit of reality, we will find the paths humanity needs in modern times, especially since they have been abandoned by those priding themselves on being practical. However, those are not truly practical people, but rather impoverished people, who brutally impose their impoverishment on the rest of us. The only way out of this difficult situation is to find the spirit, and thus reality.

In conclusion, what I wanted to emphasize in this talk is that we must develop a feeling for the relationship between our soul and the world, a feeling that emerges from the basic mood of our soul in spiritual science. Indeed, this basic mood is even more important than the various facts of spiritual science because it accompanies us throughout our whole life once spiritual science has kindled it within us.

4

SIGNS OF THE TIMES: EAST, WEST, AND CENTRAL EUROPE

ULM, APRIL 30, 1918

M y dear friends, we're gathered here to celebrate the establishment of the Ulm branch of our Anthroposophical Society. Our friends here in Ulm began meeting some time ago to pursue the endeavors and impulses of our spiritual movement in their city, and today many of us have come from out of town in honor of this event.[†] Our friends have joined forces together in difficult times, in hard times that speak to us in significant signs, and so today we will also be mindful of the larger context, the spiritual context of human development, in which our spiritual science must find its place now and in the future. Let us turn our mind, then, from our immediate spiritual interests to the all-encompassing events with which our movement is closely connected. As we know, when we join forces in the name of our spiritual impulses, our heart and soul must be imbued with the feeling that no other spiritual movement of our time can give us what we seek, what we must seek for our soul now and in the near future if we want to become fully aware of what it means to be human. Our seeking in this spiritual movement has many opponents who believe they must protect the true treasures of human development from what they consider an aberration of the human spirit, namely, from our movement. In particular, many religious or seemingly religious people feel that our movement takes people away from immersing themselves in religion.

In response we could ask whether the representatives of Christianity in the last few centuries have been able to lead humanity to a point at which the current terrible catastrophe would have been, if not prevented, at least mitigated. Admittedly, this is a rather facile judgment, but it applies nonetheless. Of course, Christianity has not been able to achieve anything like that, but people who don't want to learn from events also don't learn anything from the fact that religion as they understand it has spread for centuries, indeed, even millennia, and yet the current catastrophe has descended upon the whole world. Obvious though the above question is, let us now turn our mind in a different direction and ask a different question, one that is often neglected even though it is connected with very deep concerns of our time.

For instance, what is the word of which contemporary scholars and philologists still don't know the origin and derivation? What is the word for which you will find no definition or etymology in even the most learned reference works? This word, which we're looking for in vain in the usual scholarly sources, is the word "God." None of the sciences can tell us anything about the linguistic and spiritual origins of this word. This is very peculiar and not just a matter of outer knowledge, of factual information; rather, it is a sign of something connected on the deepest level to our mind and soul. People think they're saying something meaningful when they speak about the divine, about their devotion to God. However, even with all the resources of modern scholarship, they have not been able to explain the origin and derivation of the word "God." This shows that despite all their talk about religion and spirit most people really don't know what they're talking about. It is essential that we look more closely at what it means to say that people don't know what they're talking about, precisely when they think they're talking about what is most intimately connected with the innermost striving of the human soul. Those who have a sense for this, even if only a vague and not fully conscious one, are the ones who, amidst the spiritual confusion of our present time, feel drawn to the spiritual impulses of our movement. These impulses of anthroposophical spiritual science, as I've repeatedly emphasized while the current devastating tempest was brewing, are closely related to the most urgent needs of our time.

In particular, I want to remind you of what I have often said and what those of you who have been with our society for several years have already heard, namely, that over the course of the last three or four centuries the earth's various nations and peoples have become one in terms of commerce, industry, banking, and so on. Modern means of mass transportation ultimately have made globalization of the economy and uniformity of physical earthly life possible. For example, a check written in New York can be cashed in Tokyo or Berlin or anywhere else in the world. When I've talked about this in the years before the war, I've always added that our human body is not the only one that needs a soul; every body must have a soul and cannot live without one. The economic and industrial life that has spread like a physical body all over the globe also needs a soul, one that will allow us to understand each other spiritually as well as we do economically and financially. Thus, as I have often stressed, we must strive to give the earth body an earth soul.† This does not happen overnight but takes time, and I don't mean to criticize our time, just to describe it, so as to kindle in your soul impulses of action, thinking, feeling, and willing. I don't want to assign blame but to point out what needs to happen. Thus, I'm not blaming anyone by stating that as this shared earth body was developing so intensely in the past few decades, people have failed to develop a shared earth soul for it. There cannot be such an earth soul unless we all understand that just as everyone shares in the light of the sun, so we have something in common that unites us spiritually, and bringing this realization and understanding to people everywhere is the mission of anthroposophical spiritual science. So far we have not succeeded in this.

Our current catastrophic times show in terrifying detail, as never before in recorded history, that humanity has come to a dead end. To get out of this impasse we must get serious about adding a true spiritual culture to the physical one we're all so proud of. The culture of the earth soul is vital for our times, and for the near future, and must go hand in hand with our physical culture. People may try to resist these efforts to give earth a new spirituality, but the truth will reveal itself no matter what. We are now living in the midst of a terrible catastrophe, and if we cannot adopt this new spirituality, such catastrophes will descend upon us again and again, perhaps at shorter and shorter intervals. This catastrophe and its consequences cannot be healed with the means already available to us before this war—to believe otherwise is to ignore humanity's development on earth. Quite the contrary, the catastrophes will continue—albeit perhaps interrupted by a few years of relative tranquility—until we begin to interpret them in the only right way, that is, as signs calling us to turn toward the spirit, the spirit that must permeate our physical life. As harsh and difficult as this may seem, it is nevertheless the truth.

During the past three or four centuries of intensely proliferating materialistic culture, our connection to the spiritual world was essentially maintained by only one fact of serious significance for humanity, as those familiar with these things can attest. For instance, one of the leading representatives of the useless Society for Ethical Culture told me he'd thought long and hard about how churches still manage to exist in our enlightened times when people know that their salvation lies in understanding the material world.[†] He couldn't understand why we still have churches in addition to nations. The answer he came up with—which he held to be the expression of a deep secret—was that while nations deal with life, churches handle death, and since people still adhere to the belief that death is terrible, the churches' power is based on managing death. This is a very materialistic way of thinking and claims that once people break the habit of considering death a significant intervention in human life and begin accepting it the way animals do, then the churches would lose their power. Of course, this is nonsense, albeit brilliant nonsense. However, from the perspective of spiritual science we can see a grain of truth in it, and in our time people sometimes have to talk nonsense to express their understanding of their spiritual nature. Future generations will consider this one of the peculiarly outstanding features of our time and will describe the years from the late nineteenth to the early twentieth century—our age—as one in which the most brilliant minds had to talk nonsense if they wanted to characterize their time. However, even in nonsense there is a grain of truth; in this case it is that indeed many people are connected to the spiritual world only through their fear of death or through their dread of the notion that their loved ones who have passed away are in a sort of nothing, a void. We should not deny that these thoughts are still meaningful enough and are still connected with the most profound concerns of our soul, but neither fear nor any other feeling about death can by itself truly connect us to the spiritual world. Such a connection requires true insight into, and understanding of, the spiritual world, and we cannot achieve this unless we add to our natural scientific orientation a spiritual-scientific one.

We have to wonder what people are doing when they talk about the divine, about the need for this or that religious worship, when they claim to be so religious, and when they pray and worship the highest being—all without knowing anything about the origins of the word "God." It is indeed not irrelevant to ponder this question in a moment of serious reflection, for it implies asking who this God is that those claiming to be religious talk about. Generally, people dismiss the teachings of spiritual science about the higher beings above us, namely, the angels, archangels, archai, and others. They don't want to accept this hierarchy of spiritual beings and the great distance to the highest divine being; people don't want to muster the humility to see themselves at such a low level in the overall hierarchical context. As many have said, people don't want any intermediaries between themselves and God, but want to address God directly. However, it doesn't matter what we think about communing with God; what matters is solely what we're actually doing and experiencing in our soul. For example, what preachers of whatever religious denomination say these days about the divine applies, regardless of their actual words, in reality only to the preacher's guardian angel and not to any higher being. Of course, such a guardian angel watches over each of us throughout our life, and these preachers thus are worshipping their guardian angel but calling it by the name of the highest God. If we know what can really be contained in words, we'll see clearly that everything modern preachers say about God can never apply to any being higher than an angel, or if not to an angel, then to another entity.

Let's look at where the feelings come from that people have when they talk and preach about God or even claim to have had a direct experience of God in their soul—these days many people report such experiences and then, with a certain arrogance, call themselves "evangelized" or "born again." The soul impulse at the root of all this is their awareness of their own spiritual being as it has developed in the purely spiritual realm between their previous death and their rebirth into this life, a spiritual being now living in their body. Indeed, much of what we now meet with in our life comes originally from this inner spiritual being that developed before birth and that we now experience as a spiritual being we are at one with. People think that feeling themselves united—at one—with God is important, and even some so-called theosophists have repeatedly told people, in part to butter them up spiritually, that what matters is for people to become one inwardly with their God. Quite the contrary, what people feel when they supposedly become one with their God is only themselves, their own spiritual and soul nature as it has developed between the previous death and rebirth into this life. Thus, what pastors and priests really refer to when they talk about the God they feel in their soul is really nothing other than their own "I," which they perceive not as it now is here in the physical world in our physical body, but as it has developed in the spiritual world before birth. That is what they become aware of, and then they begin to pray—and essentially pray to themselves. Indeed, it is heart-breaking to see what's happening in so many spiritual movements of our time, especially when we have to admit that people, largely without knowing it, have begun to pray to and worship themselves.

Only rarely do people realize what's going on, and those who do often express their insight in very strange ways—Friedrich Nietzsche exemplifies this very well.[†] Ultimately, people who refuse to accept the existence of the spiritual hierarchies in all their vastness and magnificence end up praying merely to their angel or to themselves, both of which are really forms of egotistical worship. We see here the spiritual egotism humanity has gradually come to under the influence of modern materialism. You may want to object here that all this is not true, that people never speak of praying to their angel or to themselves. True, they never say so, but they do it nevertheless. The words they say are primarily intended to distract and numb themselves so they don't have to face what is really going on—which is nonetheless real, whether they are aware of it or not. In fact, the chief purpose of so much that people are saying these days is to numb and stupefy everyone because people don't want to admit to themselves what is happening. At the root of this is that many people find doing the inner work to reach spiritual worlds too inconvenient, and so they don't want to do it. Instead, they want to advance to the spiritual worlds by a much easier route than is possible, and as a result, they delude and numb themselves.

However, numbing oneself has consequences; we can't get away with it. The world runs its course, and the divine-spiritual is at work in it whether people realize it or not. Indeed, the most profound task of our time is to recover the connection to the true spiritual realm and to rid ourselves of the spiritual egotism I've described, to overcome it once and for all. We will be resolved in our hearts to accomplish this once we've really understood the true and profound impulse of spiritual science. As I have already pointed out earlier, the powerful signs the world confronts us with will undoubtedly compel people to seek the spirit again. To ensure success, though, a certain core number of people must undertake the spiritual striving that is the only right and true way for our time.

As you know, our earth has already completed several tasks; like each of us, the earth as a whole also has its task to fulfill. For example, in the epoch following the great Atlantean catastrophe, the Indian culture had a certain task to accomplish and in a later epoch the Persian culture had a different task.[†] Likewise, people dominated by the Egyptian and Chaldean cultures had a different task than those under Greek and Roman rule, a dominion that lasted until well into the fifteenth century. We are part of the epoch that began in the fifteenth century, and our task in turn is different from all the preceding ones. It will not be finished until the fourth millennium, and to describe this task we must point to the essential and fundamental events taking place on earth during this time. If we study the time before the fifteenth century from the perspective of spiritual science, we'll find that up to that time everything people did was permeated by a certain spirituality. The external discipline of history does not tell us anything about that, for it is ultimately only a fabrication we've been taught in school and college. A true and close study of those times reveals that people's everyday life was infused with a certain spirituality. The decline of that spirituality since then is one of the typical characteristics of our time; indeed, that spirituality will gradually vanish completely unless we add new spiritual impulses to our purely external, material culture. In other words, the outer conditions have forced our earth's development to become purely materialistic, and while in earlier epochs the spirit was simply there by itself, now it is up to humanity to join the spirit to what we find in the world and to do so in a free inner deed.

If we disregard for now what we can bring into earthly culture out of our own inner freedom and consciousness and instead focus only on what unfolds on its own in our epoch—which began in the fifteenth century and is the fifth one—we'll see that in this epoch the earth is beginning to die, to pass away, as far as the cosmos, the whole universe, is concerned. In other words, the fifth epoch is the beginning of earth's dying. In all preceding epochs, the earth could contribute something out of itself to the spirit of the universe described above. In contrast, the brilliant culture that developed in our epoch, in the fifth epoch—such as the telegraph, telephone, and railroad—while highly significant for the earth, has no meaning for the universe beyond our earth. For example, none of the creations and discoveries of ancient Egypt and ancient Greece will perish with the earth; however, everything that has developed in our epoch on the basis of our purely materialistic culture will pass away when the earth itself dies and becomes a world corpse. Everything our current materialistic culture has created and will still create will perish when the earth dies. This may sound sad, but our epoch had to come, inevitably, for we are meant to be free. That is, we have to be free to seek the spirit out of our inner consciousness, rather than be compelled to seek it, and therefore the current epoch had to come, in which all the outer things that we're so proud of really exist only for the earth but not for the spiritual world. Thus, our epoch has set us free to move toward the spirit, and in the process directs us to our inner life, our soul and heart. This epoch does not force us to become more spiritual, but leaves us free to choose: either to seek the spirit or to degenerate and be doomed together with the outer, material culture.

You can find this insight, which is truly essential for humanity, through spiritual science; indeed, everything in our literature gives you clues and evidence for arriving at what I've just summarized. Alternatively, after the proper preparation through spiritual science, you can see these things spelled out in the powerful signs of the times all around us—signs that are unfortunately still all too often ignored. For example, if you've studied human development in the last few decades, you'll have found, strangely enough, that there has been lively spiritual striving and activity and a widespread agreement that things must change in the area we usually call socialist, namely, in the world of workers, in the labor movement. That is where most of the recent efforts for spiritual renewal and the search for ideals for the future can be found. This movement pursues the right ideals—albeit purely materialistic ones—ideals that keep asking how the world must be transformed, how something new can arise.

Our spiritual movement is still very small and really only a small band of seekers—a crotchety, half-crazy bunch, as people often say- and thus is not part of our culture's inquiries into spiritual strivings. But if we look in other areas besides socialism for spiritual efforts, if we look at learned and clever people who have a good grasp of the ideas of our time, we find a vast spiritual wasteland. For example, theologians have engaged in the most peculiar debates, arguing about whether Christ Jesus ever lived, whether he was an extraterrestrial being, or whether he really was just a "simple man from Nazareth."† Aside from such discussions, what we find in the epoch when people have supposedly freed themselves of their "blind faith in authority" and have adopted the principle "investigate everything and keep only the best" in all their decisions is nothing other than blind faith in the alleged demands of science. What we find everywhere these days is blind faith in every scientific discipline, from history to medicine. One reason for this is that it's too much trouble for most people to learn much about what makes us healthy or sick, and so they leave it to the authorities or experts in the field. That's the most egregious blind faith in authority. In other words, for the sake of convenience, people cling to the scraps they have salvaged from the past rather than making any effort based on the realization that a spiritual renewal of humanity is absolutely essential.

In contrast, from the perspective of spiritual science we can see a new spirit being heralded in Eastern Europe, amidst the flames, so to speak, as a result of purely natural processes. Against the backdrop of the most ignominious external yoke of tyranny, the future is emerging in the minds of the Eastern European people, indeed, even in the dull and lethargic ones. Interestingly, since the ninth century the bulk of Europe has been pushing eastward all those things that should have been preserved and protected against erosion by the West.[†] Later, those things then appeared in the outward form of the Russian empire throughout several centuries, a form that preserved the old and prepared the new, future culture much like a chrysalis prepares for its emergence while still encased in its shell. In a sense, the mystery cults have survived among the Russian people; they still live with ideas of mystery and have understood very little of the abstract religious concepts so cherished in the West. Instead, the Russian people sense deep within themselves much of the cult forms and images that can lead humanity to the divine. People in Eastern Europe feel in their own soul what gives the Western religious ruler his name of pontifex, a word that means "maker or builder of bridges"; that is, he is the bridge to the spiritual realm. In other words, in Eastern Europe people have preserved as much of the old as necessary to keep the bridge to the spirit clear of the new materialism, to keep it open.

Looking at the signs of our times in connection with what I've just explained, you can't fail to see the irony, the bitter irony of human development that has been poured out over Eastern Europe in particular. Bitter irony indeed. What has spread over the region's people like a badly fitting garment is nothing but a caricature of humanity's highest and most noble strivings—that is what Leninism and Trotskyism essentially are.[†] In the final analysis they are merely the ultimate, exaggerated consequence and expression of the purely materialistic socialist ideas. Never before has there been such a clash of opposites as we see in the collision of the Eastern European soul and the inhumane Trotskyism or Leninism. I am not saying this because

I am for or against this or that, but because it is an insight showing us what terrible things are brewing in Eastern Europe as a result of the fusion of the greatest opposites that have ever merged. This insight also teaches us about the meaning of the signs of the times; it tells us that we must be serious about spiritual science and use it as a way to enter into reality. Indeed, spiritual science is first and foremost a way for us to engage with the reality of our times.

Now, Rabindranath Tagore has given a peculiar talk to a Japanese audience about the spirit of Japan.† Tagore, of course, speaks as a man from the Orient, but nowadays Europeans can easily understand people from the Orient if they want to. If we listen closely to what Tagore said about the spirit of Japan, and wanted to tell the whole world, we find that, like all people of the Orient with any understanding, Tagore knows that the Eastern peoples have preserved an ancient spiritual culture. Though the wise men of the Orient have long kept this spiritual culture secret and have not shared it with ordinary people, it has nevertheless been incorporated into their social institutions up to the present day. This culture, though spiritual to the core, has now come to the end of its time. That is why what we encounter practically all over the Asian Orient is so strangely unnatural; people there adopt Western ways of thinking, Western culture, and add it to their ancient spiritual ways. This can only lead to dire results because spiritual thinking—especially that developed by the Japanese—immerses itself in reality; and if it unites with Euro-American materialism, it will outstrip this European materialism if the latter does not become spiritualized, for Europeans have not developed the spiritual mobility that the Japanese still have as a legacy of their ancient spirituality.

Miraculously, we might say, the Russian folk soul has been spared everything leading to darkness and decadence, and Leninism and Trotskyism are now threatening to contaminate it, to infect that folk soul with the very thing that would completely eliminate the spirit from all earthly culture if it ever came to power. Obviously, that must not happen, but to prevent it and achieve spiritual victory requires that we make up our minds to no longer treat spiritual science as just another abstract theory. Spiritual science is not a convenient method for developing a certain inner delight and mystical dreaminess in our soul; it's not about making us feel good by pretending we have nothing to do with the world and can safely retreat into a spiritual beyond. Such self-satisfied disdain for the perfidious world out there is nothing but crass egotism decked out in a noble costume. We should stay away from this kind of mysticism and theosophy and instead focus only on a spiritual understanding of life, one that really comprehends and experiences the spirit and immerses itself in the world by way of this spirit. We must realize that what is involved here is a serious task for our time, albeit perhaps an unsettling and inconvenient one. It is to save people from being unsettled that certain brotherhoods have kept inconvenient truths secret from the masses. However, the time for secrets is over now; the time has come now for people to freely seek the spirit out of their inner consciousness. What has been kept secret for thousands of years must now be imparted to all people.

In other words, the spiritual wisdom that existed in ancient epochs in the Orient is now superseded and must be replaced by a different spiritual wisdom. Many people want to deny this, as we can see from the great number of so-called teachers who wanted to make things easy for us Europeans, to show us the easy answer to our quest for the spirit. Our spiritual science seems to them much too difficult because it calls for thinking—and thinking is so inconvenient, after all. Spiritual science also demands that we are spiritually awake—and being awake is so much trouble, after all. Accordingly, so-called teachers have appeared to spare us Europeans all this inconvenience and the trouble of finding our own way to the spirit; instead, they have brought us all sorts of oriental wisdom, Zarathustrian wisdom, and much else besides. As you can imagine, Europeans for the most part were very comfortable when they didn't have to find the spirit on their own but could have it brought in ready-made from ancient India. What they received worked much like a narcotic; it was a way to avoid having to seek the spirit and ultimately, by way of the spirit, the cosmos. People wanted to numb themselves and used an ancient model of knowledge for that purpose. That was one mistake people made where the East is concerned.

A second mistake was also made, namely, in connection with the fact that in our modern times the earth is, in a sense, dying in its culture, and this makes it necessary for us, even though we're not conscious of it, to seek our own inner life. And, indeed, we have this urge to find our own inner life, no doubt about it. In fact, more and more people are very eager to find their own inner life, and this seeking often appears disguised as worshipping God, in which we ultimately either worship our angels or ourselves. And yet, people will more and more urgently and intensely seek their inner life; in fact, the more the natural sciences and technology take hold of our time, the more strongly and passionately will we feel the urge to find our inner life. As it happens, people often go astray in their search these days. And it is often the ones in official positions charged with seeking the spirit who pursue the search the least; instead, they're looking for the "limits of knowledge."† They are busy finding out what we cannot know about the spiritual world. In other words, these days our spiritual leaders are the ones telling us how not to advance to the spiritual world, and their followers are seeking but have no clear awareness of their search. That is one of the most striking characteristics of our epoch.

In contrast, as a deeper understanding of the human soul will show, all over the world laypersons fully engaged in the struggles and hardships of their life are seeking the soul. Our leaders should instruct us from their pulpits and lecterns how to satisfy our seeking, but instead they claim that science forbids us to go beyond the limits of human knowledge and thus we cannot penetrate into the spiritual world. According to these luminaries, Kant told us once and for all what the limits of human knowledge are, and those who refuse to accept this are clearly fools. Indeed, this is one of the most striking features of our time. Nevertheless, very many people, though they're not aware of it, have the urge to find their inner life, and in the long run this urge will not allow them to be satisfied with "limits of knowledge" but impel them beyond those limits.

Thus, we have not only the old, worn out culture from the East to numb and distract ourselves but the far West is also sending us a means to numb and stupefy us. Indeed, Anglo-Americanism is a modern cultural narcotic to anesthetize our urge to find the spirit within us. It is the task of Anglo-American culture to organize the material realm and spread it over the whole globe, but due to an inherent idiosyncrasy, it also numbs and distracts people in their search for the spirit with its Americanisms. This means that the more we Europeans adopt the Oriental wisdom, the more we will be anesthetized in regard to spiritual knowledge of the world. Conversely, the more Americanized we become, the more we will be distracted and numbed in our search for the true spirit, for the true "I" inside us. This is not meant as a chauvinistic harangue or a tirade about this or that world mission. Rather, we must realize this, even if only in a small way, so that we can understand our special responsibility as Central Europeans. For since the age of spiritual deepening, the age of Lessing, Herder, Goethe, and Schiller—which I described in my book *The Mystery of Man* as the forgotten echo of German intellectual and spiritual life—the Central European spirit has been called upon to help humanity overcome those two anesthetics: Orientalism and Americanism.[†]

Spiritual science can help us realize the earth's spiritual situation and the demands placed on our soul, and without it people are not likely to know what spiritual impulses Central Europe can contribute to the world. Ultimately, we need to ask ourselves whether we have proven ourselves worthy of the spiritual seeking that was started by Herder and Goethe, among others. My dear friends, spiritual science rightly recommends meditation for us, and a wonderful meditation that could already be done with young children is to read Herder's description of every sunrise as a new creation in the grand context of the world.[†] And read Herder's powerful imagery in his *Ideas on the Philosophy of Human History*—alas, all this has been forgotten. Incredibly, a few days ago a gentleman with a deep and serious interest in the intellectual life of Europe told me he'd never heard that Herder wrote about any of this.

Indeed, we've been given a task and we must realize its full extent. For example, when you hear lectures by people like Ku Hung-Ming from China or Tagore from India, you shouldn't expect that they really understand the Central European spiritual impulses.[†] They may know that Goethe lived, that a Goethe Society has been established to cultivate and preserve Goetheanism, but they'll ask "so what?" What else has been done? In recent years the Goethe Society has been looking for a director, someone to lead the society, but nobody even considered whether the right man for the position would be someone working in the spirit of Goetheanism, a man who can do something for spirituality as it must be understood now, a hundred years after Goethe. No, that's not what the society was looking for. Instead, a man was hired who used to be treasury secretary.[†] So, now we have a former treasury secretary as administrator of Goetheanism; he's the one who was chosen to represent Goethean spirituality. As you can see, it is not enough to talk about spirit, spirit, and still more spirit; rather, what matters is to penetrate reality with the insights based on our spiritual understanding; we must integrate this understanding into reality. A special task has been given to us Central Europeans, and the time to fulfill it has now come. The spiritual science we're talking about here is the continuation of what began at the turn of modern cultural and intellectual life, as I've just pointed out. In truth, the purely materialistic socialist movement should have had a spiritual counterpart instead of being left to rule the field by itself for decades. While it's never too late, we must not lose any time realizing these things so that our special task does not go unfulfilled. That is, we must realize that catchphrases and slogans will not get us anywhere; what is called for is a new spirit among all people. Unfortunately, people nowadays miss or even avoid the spirit, as numerous examples prove.

We could cite thousands of such examples but will look at only one of them. Recently, a rather strange essay by a very learned man was published in a widely read German newspaper, and in this essay the writer lambasted a book that had the misfortune to have appeared in a series entitled "Of Nature and the World of the Spirit."[†] That writer railed terribly against this little book, but the essay did not explain why he was so upset. The book deals with the development of astrology and of horoscopes, albeit in the tone of an ordinary, well-behaved university professor who will, of course, not be party to the superstition of astrology. The author ends by presenting his opinion and using Goethe's horoscope as an example. In fact, he makes fun of the topic and claims that all kinds of things could be found in that horoscope. So much for what an upright university professor of our time has to say on this subject—in fact, it's not possible to find a more upright and well-behaved university professor than the author of that book. And yet, Fritz Mauthner ranted and raved about that book and claimed it was spreading superstition.[†] So, there's Fritz Mauthner inveighing against that book without even knowing why. A few days later the author of the book published a correction in which he explains that he fully agrees with Fritz Mauthner and appreciates that Mauthner makes fun of astrology and horoscopes, something he himself had also done in his book.[†] According to that published correction, he had referred to Goethe's horoscope only to show that one can read anything into it one wants. In other words, the author of the book and Mauthner were in total agreement. The *Berlin Daily News*, where Mauthner used to be theater critic, had nothing to say in reply because it did not believe that Mauthner had misunderstood anything, and Mauthner himself also has no words of explanation. In short, here two people who were in total agreement collided angrily, and neither knew why; there was no apparent reason for this clash.

That's not unusual in our time, unfortunately, but rather typical! People don't listen anymore to what they are saying to each other, and indeed they have less and less to say to each other. But the feelings they develop, their clashes, derive ultimately not from what they say to each other; rather, people are now living completely in an unfathomable, irrational element because they have become so estranged from reality they can't find their way into it. When you think this through deeply and let yourself feel what this means, there will no longer be any doubt in your soul about the importance of spiritual science. Those who believe spiritual science is unpractical are on the wrong track entirely. The fact is that in fifty years we will build no factories and start no ventures of any kind without applying spiritual science to everything, for it alone will find the way to reality. Once we realize that all old familiar slogans lead us to a dead end, that our outer material life must be accompanied by insight into the spirit that rules the world, the new outlook will be able to really understand spiritual science. That realization will keep us from wanting egotistically to cross via the "single bridge of death" into the spiritual world; instead, we will then learn to wrest life even from death.

As we seriously study spiritual science, we may be permitted to speak about these things in an intimate circle of friends such as this. For example, I have been writing about Goethe for more than thirty years now, not in an external philological, philosophical, or otherwise learned way, but always with the intention to express in my books what Goethe would want to say to us now regarding a subject that is dear to my heart. That is, I was not interested in studying the dead Goethe; rather, I wanted to find a way to the living Goethe on the basis of his legacy. My work has been about finding the living Goethe who speaks to our souls when we know that the dead are just as alive as we are, that they live in the same world as we do—the only difference is that we are still in our body while the dead are among us in spirit.

We have to wonder whether the religious communities allow for the dead and us to truly live together. While egotistical faith in immortality can be found everywhere—and we don't want to knock it here—without spiritual science, the life of the dead cannot bear fruit. It is only through spiritual science that people will find the way to the souls they had a karmic connection to and who have crossed over into the other world while yet remaining bound to this world with thousands and thousands of threads connecting us. For it is not only our impulses—the impulses of the living—that are at work in what happens here on earth; we do not stop working for this world once we have passed through the portal of death.

As we've seen, even during our waking hours we are only partially awake, namely, in our perception and thinking. In contrast, in our feelings we are in a dreamlike state; feelings live in our awareness much like dreams do. Where our will is concerned, we're actually fast asleep. We can know our thoughts and remember our dreams, but in our ordinary consciousness we don't even know how the will works when we move our arms. In feeling we're really dreaming, and in willing we're deeply asleep. Basically, we are feeling and willing beings surrounded by a world of the spirit we cannot access with our ordinary consciousness; perception and thinking have separated us from that world. By virtue of being what we are, that is, beings who perceive and think and enjoy the physical world, we are not aware of the dead walking among us. In truth, the dead are everywhere among us. After developing in our life here, we pass through the portal of death. However, even then we remain connected with life on earth; many bonds, like fine yet strong threads, keep us linked to and involved in life on earth. In fact, there is no feeling or willing without the involvement of the dead with whom we have a karmic connection. Spiritual science allows us to realize this, to see the dead not as lives lost to us on earth, not as having vanished into nothingness, but rather as living on and working in our life here on earth. This realization is also the foundation of the spiritual orientation of the peoples in the East. In contrast, the peoples of Central Europe have the task of drawing forth from the human soul everything we can consciously create out of the freedom of our soul, a task that will last into the fourth millennium. To perform this task we must permeate the outer material world with the spiritual. At the same time, we must take care not to let the world sink into Wilsonism, which is the opposite of spirituality of any kind.[†] In the East, where Trotskyism and Leninism have been grafted onto the emerging spirituality, clashing and grating against it, the new spiritual culture being prepared must be set free. That culture is called upon to ask the vital question about everything that happens on earth: what are the dead saying about this?

Now more than ever, it is essential for us to realize that this is where we're headed in our earthly development. However, these days people think they are so smart and are already smart enough at twenty to run for parliamentary elections; after all, nowadays everyone already has a firm standpoint by age twenty and feels like a full-fledged person. What we need to understand deeply is that it's not for nothing that we're given the years between age twenty and the day we die. On the contrary, we continue to learn and develop and to discover something new all the time, and even after we've passed through the portal of death, learning and life continue. It's essential that we fully realize this. Thus, in the future, people will know that the wisest persons to ask for advice about what should be done here on earth are the dead.

Our consciousness soul—you can read what that is in my book *Theosophy*—is being formed by our present time; our spiritual self will be developed by the culture of the future. In fact, our spirit self develops as the dead become the advisors of the living. People still consider this a fantastic dream or a sort of madness, but it will nevertheless become reality. A time will come—indeed, is coming—when people who have joined together here on earth to accomplish a goal of significance for earthly development will not only consult the living but also the dead. We cannot yet go into detail about what specific form this will take and how it will be incorporated into our political structures and institutions; at this point, all of that must still remain a mystery. However, we can already immerse ourselves in the realization that this living consciousness must develop, that we are always in the company of the dead, that instead of an egotistical aspiration to immortality we should create within us a living striving that is then expressed in our actions.

In conclusion, I wanted us today to reflect on how spiritual science integrates the aspirations of each individual person into the overall striving of the earth. I thought this topic was especially appropriate for our gathering here with friends who are seeking the answers to life's questions in spiritual science. What we're talking about here is not a matter of meeting the paltry needs of our soul; rather, cultivating spiritual science is a matter of the earth culture's destiny. Becoming aware of this will not make us arrogant or conceited; we can be humble, but we must develop this awareness because it is essential now that there are people who fully understand the seriousness of human striving on earth. If you immerse yourself in spiritual science as I've indicated here today, you'll find that even a small branch of our society, such as this one, can make a contribution to the human development that is necessary if the earth is to advance toward its ultimate goal.

5

REBELLION AGAINST THE SPIRIT

HAMBURG, JUNE 30, 1918

T HERE are many ways to approach the question dear to our hearts that we have often discussed, namely, why so few people in our time have found their way to a spiritual understanding of the world order. Today, let us consider it from a point of view that will lead us to certain thoughts that may be very important for us, especially in these times. In studying humanity's relationship to the spiritual world, what interests us especially is our relationship to those human souls in our circle—souls with whom we have karmic connections—who have already passed through the portal of death and are thus already in the spiritual realm. Our relationship to the dead will always be one of the most interesting aspects of our relationship to the spiritual world, and it shows most clearly how spiritual science and the physical-sensory world differ in their understanding of the human being. As I've often pointed out, as we come to know the spiritual world, we must often radically break with our conventional notions about physical life because the terms we have to use for what happens in the spiritual world are generally the exact opposite of the ones we use for the physical world. Of course, this does not mean that simply turning the physical world upside down and reversing everything will lead us to understanding the spiritual world. That is not the case; rather, every detail must be examined and experienced individually.

Still, particularly regarding our relationship to the so-called dead, we must begin by adopting concepts and terms that are the opposite of the physical and conventional ones.

We can learn from spiritual researchers what things are like, but what they tell us about our relationship to the dead is what more or less all of us experience already, except that for most of us it remains subconscious unless we are spiritual researchers. Thus, I will be talking here today about things you all experience also; in particular, I'll be talking about the relationships to the so-called dead you are all part of already but without being aware of it. It is up to spiritual science to make us conscious of these things. Once the spiritual world has thus revealed itself to you, you'll find that in communicating with the dead we will, of course, not use words as we do with the living. Instead, we will address the dead with our thoughts. If we have a true connection with the dead soul, we'll feel that what we address to the dead in our thoughts—our questions and concerns—is coming from them. In contrast, when we ask someone a question in our physical life here, we hear ourselves speak as we address our words to the other person. Conversely, when we're talking with the dead we feel ourselves quiet, for if the dead really receive the words we address to them, and if we have a real connection to them, then our words, our thoughts, seem to come from the dead to us. The dead seem to speak to us, and what they're saying comes out of the depths of our own soul in the form of an answer or a message.

In other words, the way we communicate with the dead is the other way around from how we talk to people here in the physical world. It thus is not surprising that many people don't notice this in their ordinary life; it goes against what they're used to. By the same token, if most of us didn't have such a hard time getting used to something unfamiliar, many more of us would be able to talk about their interactions with the dead. For example, we're all always in relationships with the dead who have a karmic connection to us, and if you want to intensify and deepen this relationship, you must first understand an important rule, namely, that abstract thoughts and ideas have hardly any significance for the spiritual world. Everything that remains abstract will not reach the spiritual world. That is, if you only think abstractly of a dead soul, if you only love that soul abstractly, then not much of this will actually be received by the dead. In contrast, if you anchor your connection to the dead in something concrete, then the dead can receive your communication. To achieve this, remember a particular time when you were with that person before he or she died and recall in great detail how that person was sitting or standing or going for a walk with you. Recall the dead in concrete situations, what he or she said, what you said, and try to remember his or her tone of voice. In addition—and this is the hardest part—revive in yourself the feelings you used to have for that person, let them come to life again in your soul. Begin with a concrete, specific situation you shared and then try to say something to the dead soul, something you would want to say or ask if that person were still alive. And do this as vividly as you can, as though that person were still there with you. If you do this, you will reach the dead soul; he or she will receive what you want to say. However, this does not happen all at once as soon as you feel that you're telling or asking the dead soul something. The connection between you takes time to become established, and time has a different meaning for spiritual life than it does here in the physical world.

On the basis of what I've just explained, you can establish a real connection with a dead individual even without being a spiritual researcher. However, for your message to reach the dead, it must wait for a certain time. In general, for those without special initiation and without a conscious relationship to the spiritual world, one particular moment is especially important for establishing communication with the dead: the moment of falling asleep. The moment that carries you from the waking state into sleep generally also carries everything you have addressed to the dead in the course of the day to that person. Thus, the same path that takes you into the spiritual world as you fall asleep also takes your communications into the realm of the dead. That is why we have to be very careful in interpreting dreams; often dreams are merely reminiscences of what we experienced that day, but they can also be reflections of something real. And very often—though not always—our dreams of the dead are based on our relationship with an actual dead soul. People often—and mistakenly—believe that what appears to them in such dreams, what the dead communicates to them, is in reality just as it appears in the dream. On the contrary, the dead receives what you want to convey to him or her as you fall asleep, and what your dream shows you is how the dead received your communication. In other words, when the dead tells you something in your dream, it is an indication that your message was received. Thus, rather than believe that the dead soul appeared in your dream to tell you something, you must realize that your dream shows that what you wanted to tell a dead individual has reached that soul, and by means of the dream the dead is showing you that he or she has understood what you wanted to convey.

The moment that is especially important for receiving a message or answer from the dead is that of waking up. What the dead want to say to us is carried to us from the spiritual realm in the moment of our waking up, and we experience this rising up out of the depths of our own soul. Typically, however, people don't like to pay attention to what rises up out of the depths of their soul, and this is especially true in our time. Generally, people prefer to receive impressions from the outer world and to focus on only what is in this external world, and they'd prefer to numb themselves against what comes up out of their soul. When they finally do become aware of a thought or idea rising out of their soul, they believe it as their own inspiration and thus gratify their vanity. We tend to think of everything that comes up out of our depths like this as our own idea, our own inspiration—and occasionally that may even be true. For the most part, however, the inspirations and ideas that come up out of our own depths are actually the answers the dead are sending to us. In fact, the dead are living closely together with us, and what seems to speak out of your own depths is really what the dead are telling you. Therefore, it is essential that we interpret this experience in the right way. I've already told you about the details of communicating with the dead: for example, reading aloud to them, and so on. The more vividly, feelingly, and imaginatively you enter into these things, the more meaningful your relationship with the dead will be.

It is very important to clearly understand this, for in our time the truth about these things is needed more than ever. We're living in an era in which our organism is in decline, a decline that began a long time ago. As a result, our body cannot express how spiritual and wise we really are. In ancient Greece people's bodies reflected and expressed their spiritual nature, but since about the middle of the Atlantean period, the human body has been in decline, a condition that has by now advanced to such an extent that our spiritual nature can no longer be expressed in our body. Accordingly, we find frequently that at death we have not yet completed, so to speak, our development. If only people would properly understand this! We're developing throughout our life, but we can only become aware of that part of our development that is reflected in our body. Some of us are already very wise at the time of their death, and could still provide valuable services both to the earth and to the spiritual realm, but their declining body cannot reveal these things to them and make them usable. However, once we establish a relationship with the dead in the way I've described, we can make use of those services. In fact, the dead want to continue their activity and contribution to physical life, but they can do so only by way of human souls that open themselves to the dead in the right way.

As I've probably told you before, this issue is dear to my heart; for example, I don't think of my work as continuing where Goethe left off, as studying him and his worldview in terms of history or literary history. Rather, I've always been convinced that I'm not just dealing with the Goethe who died in 1832 but with the one living at the end of the nineteenth and the beginning of the twentieth century. What I'm interested in is the living Goethe; though he took much away with him when he left the physical world in 1832, he can still work on in our world if we could only realize it. Accordingly, my books are not merely the result of research in literary but rather they convey what he has told me. However, contemporary culture, our so-called spirit of the age, is completely opposed to what I've just told you.

Spiritual science must always be involved in life and bear fruit for our life. In our time an ideal is gaining ground, however, that goes totally against what I've described as a peculiarity of this era. This ideal is evident in people's continued striving to have as little faith in life as possible. Essentially, people have faith in life only until they are in their twenties, as their practical goals already indicate. In contrast, in ancient Greece people still believed that they would be wiser in their old age than in their youth, that older people would know more about state and city politics than young. This faith has been abandoned, for nowadays most people want to reduce the age at which they're eligible to stand for parliamentary elections as far as possible because they have faith in life only until their early twenties. However, life demands of us that we have faith in it as a whole, that we believe our development continues all through our whole life. Imagine how differently we would relate to each other if we knew that we're developing throughout our whole life, how differently young people would treat their elders if they were steeped in this realization. Imagine the moral impulses and the different quality of consciousness you would have if you knew at every stage of your life that you're just a greenhorn, for example, at thirty or thirty-five, and that getting older is a thing of hope because you expect it will bring you something that you cannot have in your youth. Just imagine with what zest for life and vitality you'd live if this realization would permeate your whole life. Then even just before your death, you would see that you can't advance far enough in this life to reflect everything life offers you into your consciousness, and so you'll decide to carry something of that through death into the next life, and people who believe in the dead will then approach you and allow you to advise and counsel them. Well, as you can imagine, these days we're considered stupid and foolish when we proclaim this truth, which has to become a practical principle in human life in the future. Seriously, all parliaments the world over would make wiser decisions if the dead were advising them. That is, decisions and laws would be better, if in addition to the opinions of greenhorns in their thirties, people would also consider what Goethe, for example, or other dead individuals older than a hundred years would say about the issues at hand. This way of thinking must become a practical reality in the future.

These days, certain so-called secret societies make much of preserving and using many ancient symbols. In truth, they would do better to work on understanding their own time and to devote themselves to researching the advice of the dead—that would be so much more important and meaningful. For humanity cannot advance unless it is steeped in the realization that the divine-spiritual realm works in our development throughout our whole life; we're not finished developing when we've reached our twenties.

As I've pointed out before, in ancient times people could still feel their soul and spirit developing as they felt the physical development of their body over the course of their life. That is, in very ancient times people felt the development of their soul and spirit going along with and, indeed, dependent on that of their physical body, and they felt that way into their forties and fifties. Nowadays, people feel the soul-spiritual development going hand in hand with the physical one only up until puberty, or at most into their early twenties. However, if we remain capable of development beyond that, we'll find that around age thirty-five, as our physical body begins to decline, our spiritual forces develop particularly strongly, but only if we have allowed them to sprout with the help of spiritual science. In the past, older people were respected and revered because everyone realized that they knew something that could not yet be revealed to the younger generation. As I've pointed out before, these days humanity is getting ever younger. For example, in the ancient Indian culture people remained capable of development well into their fifties, and in the ancient Persian culture they continued developing into their forties. In contrast, in the Egypto-Chaldean culture this development lasted until people were in the second half of their thirties and in the Greco-Roman culture until they reached age thirty-five. When the Greco-Roman culture came to an end in the fifteenth century, people remained capable of development only until age twenty-eight, and today the period of development ends at age twenty-seven.

Based on these insights, the prototypical individual of our time is one who completely refuses any soul impulse toward spiritual development—who only accepts what comes to him from the outer world, from what the present time offers. In other words, the person who unites all the characteristics of our era in himself is one who has not attended an intellectual lyceum where pupils study the past and receive impulses for their soul development. Instead, such a prototypical person has merely taken in the impressions from the outer world, that is, the sensations and feelings we can experience in the present. He is a self-made man, and from seven, eight, or nine years of age he grows up with a certain aversion to the privileged classes. He is the sort of person who will not raise his hat to people with aristocratic titles or any other sort of power. Accordingly, he does not attend a school where Greek and Latin are taught but instead learns from life itself. Eventually, he gets a kind of lawyer-type job, again not by studying for the bar but by struggling through practical training in a law office. Until age twenty-seven he takes in whatever the present time brings him, that is, nothing that is taken from revisiting the culture of the past. By age twenty-seven he would have to stand for parliamentary elections and then present himself to his contemporaries much the way he has developed himself until that point: as a self-made man with no faith in further development. Once elected to parliament, he can then run for a ministerial post. According to the current prevailing opinion, development would be completely out of place in such a position because if the candidate developed further, people might see any changes in his views as contradictions and accuse him of being inconsistent and fickle. That is, once elected to parliament, politicians must stick to their opinion and can't change it if they don't want to be accused of flip-flopping. You may wonder if such a prototypical person actually exists—indeed, he does; his name is Lloyd George.[†] Of course, people's idiosyncrasies, their true inner nature, cannot be understood unless we examine it from the perspective I've presented here. Then we will see that Lloyd George is a self-made man and until age twenty-seven has taken in only what our present time provides, and because he lacks any impulse for soul development, he stops taking in anything new at that age. At that age he's elected to parliament, where he takes his place, sitting with his arms folded across his chest and his eyes turned slightly inward, and speaks very much to the point while watching his opponents closely for any signs of weakness.

Then, in the Campbell-Bannerman administration the question was what to do with Lloyd George, a man who criticizes everything the administration does.[†] So, what solution was decided on? It was decided to make Lloyd George a minister and thus part of the administration, a position from which he can't mount much of an opposition anymore.

Accordingly, Lloyd George takes the ministerial post and in very short order fully adapts to his new role and is at home in it; after all, he is a true representative of our time. Of course, the question then was what portfolio to entrust to him based on his talents and abilities. And after some deliberation, it was decided to give a portfolio he didn't know anything about: that of public works. But, lo and behold, within only three months he had become thoroughly familiar with that area and has since done great things as minister of public works, a field he had known nothing about before.

You see, that Lloyd George clearly typifies our time, and he's not the only such figure. All of them have taken in everything their surroundings offer until their twenty-seventh year—that's the cutoff point—and have then entered public life and stopped developing further. One of those figures you may be more familiar with is Matthias Erzberger, whose biography is remarkably similar to that of Lloyd George once we study the two in the esoteric way I've explained here.† It's an odd historical phenomenon, and the esoteric study of the human soul must become part of humanity's future development for a true understanding of the culture of our era. Indeed, our time in particular demands of us to delve more deeply into these things that most people are uncomfortable with. To meet this demand of our time, we must allow the dead a voice in our decisions—a fact that will, of course, be rejected outright by those people who most typify our time.

In contrast, to study a person who embodied the ongoing striving for further development and the unconscious faith that a divine-human reality lives in us until death, we have to look at Goethe, who typified all this even more than is generally believed. Goethe's aim was twofold: to take in what the outer world offered in his early years and also to continue developing. In *Dichtung und Wahrheit* (Autobiography: Truth and Fiction Relating to My Life) he described his early years up to the move to Weimar.† Born in 1749, Goethe moved to Weimar in 1775; that is, his memoirs cover the first twenty-six years of his life and end shortly before his twenty-seventh because he knew unconsciously that this is an important turning point. These days we experience a similar turning point at age thirty-five, but most of us sleep right through it. This is the moment when our rising, unfolding life begins to decline as far as the physical body is concerned, and precisely then our spirit is compelled to reveal itself more and more. Clearly, our thirty-fifth year is a very important one; it is the year we give birth to our soul in our physical body. For Goethe, who retained the capacity for further development throughout his life, this meant that shortly after his thirty-fifth year, in 1786, he left for Italy until age forty-two. When you study his biography more closely you'll see that this was a major turning point for him. In an essay that will now be published in a small book—the essay entitled "Goethe's Spirit as it is revealed in his *Faust* and in his Fairytale of the Snake and the Lily"—I've established Goethe's personal relationship to his *Faust*, or at least provided some indications for it.[†] Particularly in regard to this topic, much of what is generally written about Goethe is more confusing and misleading than enlightening. Many people refer with smug gravity to Faust's introductory lines:

> Have now, alas! quite studied through
> Philosophy and Medicine,
> And Law, and ah! Theology, too,
> With hot desire the truth to win!
> And here, at last, I stand, poor fool!
> As wise as when I entered school. . .[†]

People smugly and almost gleefully point out that Faust studied all four disciplines and still didn't get anywhere, but doubts all knowledge. Especially the actors studying that role often feel they must disdain the four disciplines, but that is not what is typically and characteristically Goethean here; it's only the very beginning, as many of Goethe's contemporaries used to say. When the true Goethean element appears in *Faust*, namely, when Faust picks up the book of Nostradamus and first sees the sign of the macrocosm, then things change. This symbol, after all, shows what the place of human beings in the macrocosm is. The relationship of our spirit to the spirit of the world, of our soul to the soul of the world, and of our physical body to the physical world—all that is represented in the big picture of the buckets within buckets that flow into each other, of planets and suns and the hierarchies ruling them. However, Faust turns away, saying "Majestic show! but ah! a show alone!" That is, he sees only pictures, a show or spectacle, because he wants to comprehend the mystery of the world that moment, in *one* instant. Faust wants in an instant what, in the physical world, can only be attained over the course of a lifetime, if at all. Knowledge cannot give us anything but pictures or images, and that is why Faust turns to the sign of the microcosm, where he finds not the spirit of the macrocosm but only the earth spirit, the spirit of human history on earth, that describes itself in these words:

> In life's tide currents, in action's storm,
> Up and down, like a wave,
> Like the wind I sweep!†

What Faust is seeking with the help of the earth spirit is self-knowledge, not knowledge of the world. And this is the true Goethean moment in the drama; the preceding parts are merely leading up to that point. As a young man, Goethe arrived at the conclusion that everything related to the macrocosm provides only images and remains ultimately impenetrable; however, the answer to the mystery of life can be found only inside. Thus, when the earth spirit declares,

> Thou'rt like the spirit thou canst comprehend,
> Not me!†

Faust collapses. After all, what is that spirit he resembles? *Faust* offers us the rare opportunity to study a poet who does not just theorize. Goethe does not limit himself to theory but presents vividly and artistically how things really are. Thus, the above-quoted lines are followed by Wagner's knocking and entering. In other words, here is the answer: Faust is like Wagner, not like the earth spirit. This passage in *Faust* in particular must be reconsidered; it should not be staged the way it usually is, with Faust as the man striving for higher ideals, struggling to ascend to the spirit, the man who is right at all costs—and then Wagner comes hobbling in. If I were to direct the play, I would have Wagner wear Faust's mask so that both look alike, because the point of the scene is to make Faust see "here stands your spitting image; you're no farther advanced than he is." And indeed, Wagner's lines at this point are logically consistent and make sense, while Faust's words are only about longings and yearnings. However, Faust scholars, and other people too, want to have things as easy and convenient as possible and so don't look at this scene closely enough. Thus, they like to quote Faust's lines,

All comes at last to feeling;
Name is but sound and smoke,
Beclouding Heaven's warm glow,[†]

forgetting that Faust is saying this to a sixteen-year-old girl. In other words, pearls of wisdom designed for a teenager are taken as a philosophical truth.

In this first scene, then, Wagner comes to Faust for the latter's self-knowledge—as I said, all this is explained in more detail in my little book—yet, Faust has been touched already by the spirit, for the earth spirit appeared to him. Thus, Faust has had a small taste of the spiritual world, and now he cannot rest until he advances further and makes up for what he failed to do in his first forty years. At the beginning of the play, Faust is forty years old; that is when he looks back on what he has failed to do in his youth, and sees he missed much, including the Bible. And then he encounters a different kind of self-knowledge than what Wagner offered when he meets Mephistopheles.

Something odd happened then: when in the nineties, in 1797, Schiller urged Goethe to continue his *Faust*. In 1797 Goethe was forty-eight years old, another significant moment in a person's life. Seven times seven is forty-nine, and that is the age when we move beyond the development of our own individual spirit self into the spirit of life. Schiller urged Goethe to get to work, but people have generally found an easier explanation for the facts; for example, Jakob

Minor wrote an interesting book about Goethe and explained that Goethe was simply getting old and thus no longer as capable of writing poetry.[†] However, if this were the case, then *Faust* could never be written in the first place, for then it would not be possible to represent human life in later years, and when we meet Faust in the play, he is already getting a bit long in the tooth, after all. When Goethe was struggling with continuing his *Faust*, he was at the age that the ancient Indians believed to be the age at which people are finally old enough to ascend to the realm of their forefathers and to penetrate gradually deeper and deeper into the mysteries of spiritual life. That is the moment when Goethe encountered his Mephisto in a peculiar way. As you know, there are two forces opposing us: Ahriman and Lucifer. Goethe confounded and combined them without realizing it at the time, and that is why Mephisto is an ambiguous, contradictory figure, as many details in the tragedy show. Mephisto is thus actually a combination of Ahriman and Lucifer, and Goethe did not realize this until 1797, and that's why he found it so difficult to continue his *Faust*. At that time spiritual science had not yet advanced sufficiently to be able to split humanity's opponent into two, and so Goethe used only one. We learn much about the nature of Goethe from the fact that he should have created two figures opposing Faust but instead merged the two into one, and he had to endure a certain inner turmoil regarding the contradictory character of Mephisto. That *Faust* was nevertheless completed and is a literary masterpiece is, of course, due to Goethe's poetic genius—and this, too, is something Goethe found surging up in him from out of his subconscious. From all this you can see that we can remain capable of further development beyond our twenties and that we can feel in a very elementary way in our soul what is working within us together with the spirit throughout our whole life.

Interestingly, Goethe didn't write the part of *Faust* that we know as "Prologue in Heaven" until 1798. Goethe did not explicitly say what motivated him there, but he has Faust once again pick up a book, and this time Faust encounters the spirit. It's not just a show anymore, but now Faust sees the spirits weaving in the spheres and finds himself in the midst of the macrocosmic struggle between good and evil. In other words, we should not read *Faust* as though every-thing in the tragedy were of equal significance or read the whole play with the same attitude. Instead, we can see where Goethe broke with the worldview of his youth and led Faust deeper and deeper into the spirit of the macrocosm. This also shows you how orderly and steadily Goethe's life developed and unfolded. In fact, Goethe's life shows us clearly how human life progresses toward death in developmen-tal phases of seven years each. This is one example of how we must increasingly raise the subconscious to consciousness—of course, we have to proceed in a way that is appropriate to the spirit of our time.

There's a lot of talk these days about the subconscious, but it is not properly understood or seen in the right way. Analytical psychology and psychoanalysis are trying to control and manage the subconscious spiritual-soul element in us, but with inadequate means; only spiri-tual science provides adequate means for understanding the subcon-scious. The cases psychoanalysts so often mention to explain their work reveal precisely how inadequate their approach is.[†] For example, let's assume—to use a basic psychoanalytical case—a woman meets a married man and develops a relationship with him that he liked but his wife didn't like. Lo and behold, for many reasons—among them very likely also her husband's female friend—the wife gets sick and develops various nervous troubles, as so many people do nowadays. Indeed, it's not surprising that she fell ill considering how common it is for people nowadays to develop neurasthenia. Now, the wife decides to spend a few months at a health spa to recover, and on the evening of her departure, a small dinner party is arranged to which the husband's female friend, who is essentially a friend of the whole family, is also invited. The dinner runs smoothly, and the moment arrives when the lady of the house has to leave to catch her train. The company disperses; people are going home. A group of guests, however, walks out to the street with the woman who is such close friends with the husband of the house. As often happens late at night in quiet neighborhoods, people don't stay on the sidewalk but walk in the middle of the street.

Suddenly, a carriage, a hackney cab, comes racing around the corner, and while all the others jump out of the way back onto the sidewalk, the woman who is such good friends with that husband keeps running as fast as she can in front of the horses instead. The coachman curses and yells and cracks his whip, but the woman seems oblivious and just keeps running as the horses dash after her. Finally, they come to a bridge, and she realizes the danger and in a split second decides to save herself by jumping into the river. She saves herself by jumping off the bridge. Ultimately, she is pulled out of the water and rescued. And the other guests who had followed her carry her back to the house. Because of her condition, she has to spend the night there in the house of her married friend. All the other guests leave, but she has to stay there. In this way something is brought about that I don't want to talk about in more detail now. However, psychoanalysts study this case looking for hidden psychological motives. Among other theories they consider, they also speculate that perhaps that woman had a traumatic experience with horses in her childhood, when she was seven or eight years old. Perhaps that experience reverberated through her soul and overpowered her so that she lost consciousness due to a fear of horses. This is how psychoanalysts are searching out "lost regions in the soul."

However, the truth is quite different. The truth is that our subconscious is cleverer and craftier than our consciousness, and the woman I've been telling you about was a very respectable lady, but she was in love with a married man. Her waking consciousness would not have allowed her to admit that she wanted to stay in his house, but her subconscious did so easily, and figured out to the last detail that if she keeps running in front of the horses and then jumps off the bridge, people will bring her back to that man's house. That is what she achieves by her actions that night after the carriage thunders around the corner. Of course, in her normal consciousness she would never have admitted this, but her subconscious can admit such desires and design a plan to realize them. In other words, our subconscious is much wiser and much more crafty than our rational consciousness— for better or worse.

As I've said, the subconscious is gaining some notoriety these days, but people generally employ inadequate means to approach it. We must realize that only spiritual science can give us what is needed to show that in addition to the "I" that lives in our body, we also have within us an eternal spiritual element, one that is not just angelic but can also be very cunning, depending on its karma. Spiritual science studies how the subconscious reveals itself through us, and it is now more important than ever that these things are understood as they really are, that the truth about them is known. In our time, the subconscious knocks more and more frequently on the door of our consciousness, so to speak, and we will not be able to cope well with life if we ignore the paths our subconscious takes rather than exploring them with our consciousness. Many people don't want to engage in this exploration, and that is why they shy away from spiritual science. Thus, there are several reasons why people avoid spiritual science; one is that they don't want to accept that everything is really different—upside down, so to speak—regarding our relationship with the dead. To establish and understand such relationships we have to re-think everything. For example, in ordinary life we hear the words coming out of our mouth when we say something, but when we're communicating with the dead, everything we say really flows out of the dead soul; conversely, what the dead say to us comes up from within us. All this is perfectly natural.

Another reason why people shy away from spiritual science is their antagonistic attitude to the spirit, largely because they don't want to admit how close the spiritual is to their consciousness, in how many places it is knocking at the door of our consciousness. For example, in people deviating a bit from the norm, the spiritual-soul element is relaxed and loosened in their physical body, and as a result their subconscious enters their consciousness more strongly—and in the right way—than in people without such a loosening. This doesn't mean that we should aim for such a loosening—definitely not—but it happens naturally in some people, as in Otto Weininger, for example.[†] Weininger was truly a gifted person and earned his doctorate when he was only in his early twenties. Then he reworked his dissertation into a book entitled, *Sex and Character: An Investigation of Fundamental Principles.* It is an amateurish and in many respects trivial book, but still remarkable. After completion of the book, Weininger traveled to Italy and kept a diary of his journey that is filled with all sorts of strange entries. Certain insights of spiritual science are presented there in the form of caricatures—the loosened spiritual-soul element can see and understand many things but tends to turn them into caricatures. And often we also find a certain erosion of morals in people like that. Nevertheless, Weininger was a genius. At the age of twenty-three he rented a room in the house where Beethoven used to live, and there Weininger shot himself. This shows that he was quite abnormal.

In his last book there is a strange passage in which Weininger explains that people don't remember their life before birth because the soul has become so degenerate that it wants to lull itself into unconsciousness where the previous life is concerned.[†] I mention this example—and I could cite thousands more—to show you that there are many people who are actually very close to spiritual science but still cannot find their way to it because our modern world doesn't want people to come to spiritual science. Weininger is an ideal example because in him the spiritual-soul element was loosened enough so he could accept as a mater of course that within us a spiritual-soul nature unites itself with our physical body. That is, Weininger could take for granted and talk about what many people nowadays can speak about only bashfully, if at all. And developing such courage and strength to face the spiritual world in all its concrete forms is indeed one of our fundamental tasks in our time.

One such concrete form that I wanted to talk about especially is that we need to let the dead have a say in our life. In addition, it is essential that how we live together is shaped by the differences we feel among ourselves based on age, by the realization that we change as we age. On that basis we can then develop faith in our life as a whole. After all, God does not stop revealing himself to us once we are out of our twenties. In earlier times that revelation was a physical one, but now we must feel our way to God through spiritual science. For this, it is essential that we believe in the gifts from the divine-spiritual world and are supported inwardly through our whole life by the encouraging sense that as we get older, we can bring something to the divine-spiritual realm that it can then accept differently than it did before. As you can imagine, it will make a great difference to be able to approach the future with such hope and expectation.

Indeed, our whole way of living together, our social structures, will be as though covered with a new soul-spiritual aura—an aura we urgently need as we prepare for the future. All this is of the utmost importance; therefore, let yourself fully feel and absorb how urgently changes must come. Our time demands that many things change; in particular, we must let go of our old hypocritical way of seeing things and instead see them for what they really are. It's pointless to deceive ourselves with lies about anything, and now I'd like to talk about one such self-deception in particular.

These days many people claim to revere and worship not the various hierarchies—the angels, archangels, and so on—but what they call "my God," and they pride themselves on what they call humanity's great progress in having arrived at monotheism, the faith in one god. However, we cannot help but wonder who people are really turning to in their attempts to establish a concrete relationship to the spiritual world and who they mean by "my God." Whether Catholic or Protestant, when we talk about God we all refer only to what our consciousness can actually comprehend, namely, to one of two things: our guardian angel or our own "I." That is, in actuality we're worshipping our guardian angel—each of us has one with the task to protect us—and calling it God. Or we're worshipping our own "I," all the while deceiving ourselves, because every one has his or her unique angel, and we call all of them—or our own unique "I"—by the same name, that of God. In this context it's important to remember that the one word whose origin we don't know despite all our research is that very word "God." That's food for thought and should interest us very much. You can look up the word in all kinds of dictionaries that offer linguistic and philological background information on words, and you'll find there's no certainty or consensus about the word "God." In other words, people don't know what they mean by the word "God." Essentially, they can only mean either their angel or their own "I"; in the latter case, they become unconscious followers, so to speak, of our spiritual science because they're actually talking about their "I" as it has developed in the period between their previous death and the birth into their current life. Concretely, then, people use the name God either for their angel—it's only an angel but they call it God—or for their own individual "I." No matter how we try to reinterpret this, basically we find such an egotistical religion in many souls these days, but people don't want to admit it. Ultimately, spiritual science alone will make this clear to us, and as a result people will hate spiritual science and fight it because they find it convenient to call what is directly above them in the hierarchical order by the name of God. Basically, all the talk about God these days is really only about people's own "I" or their angel.

To get beyond this mistaken view of the hierarchies, we must adopt spiritual science in a concrete way, and this will become ever more urgent and important to understand as we prepare for the future. Above all, we must have truth—truth will be even more important in the future than now, and indeed we don't find much truth in our times. Truth is a rare commodity these days. Particularly in scholarly disciplines some strange notions of truth prevail. For example, as I've described in my book *Riddles of the Soul*, if I may mention this here briefly, Max Dessoir, a rather peculiar fellow, has a strange way of dealing with the truth.[†] Reading about him in the most recent issue of the *Kant Studies* can break one's heart; I can talk about this because Anthroposophy isn't mentioned at all in that essay, and thus it does not hurt us.[†] Nevertheless, it is sad to find an essay that is so amateurish and banal—not just where Anthroposophy is concerned, but through and through—in that "scholarly" journal, and see that it is taken seriously.

As I've explained in my book, we can prove step by step—indeed, with Dessoir that's the only way possible—that he has not read my books but misrepresents and perverts them. To mention just one of the most stupid distortions, in the first edition of his book *Vom Jenseits der Seele* (From the Far Side of the Soul) Dessoir claims that my *Philosophy of Freedom* was my first book.[†] As you know, that book was published in 1894, ten years after my first book. This just goes to show how perfunctory and careless Dessoir is, not just on this subject, but in everything. Among more important things, I've also pointed out this mistake to him to show him his carelessness. Now, in the preface to the second edition of his book Dessoir explains a number of things that show what kind of person this university professor really is. For example, he claims that in his first edition he didn't mean to say that *The Philosophy of Freedom* is my first book but only that it is my first theosophical book. When you consider this claim in light of how other people see that same *Philosophy of Freedom* as repudiated by my "theosophy," you'll get a glimpse of the quagmire all around us. Such things are very revealing and show us clearly the true nature of our present time. It is obviously of the utmost importance to understand these things, and we can do so only if we openly arm ourselves with the weapons of spiritual science.

Among other things, spiritual science will change our approach to history, for history as conventionally taught is actually nothing more than a fabrication. Once we really understand the facts based on our spiritual science, we will find that they are quite different from what the history textbooks want to make us believe. For example, just to mention one point—please bear with me, it will be clear to you later where I'm going with this—we know that the fourth post-Atlantean epoch ended in the fifteenth century; that is, the last remnants of the Greco-Roman period vanished some time in the 1400s. In 1413, at a major historical turning point, the fifth post-Atlantean epoch began. In light of these facts, we have to wonder what caused the fall of the Roman Empire, the last stronghold of Greco-Roman culture. There are many causes, but one of the most important is the following. As you know, the Romans waged many extensive wars that gradually expanded the empire's territory beyond its initial borders. As a result, more and more peoples and ethnic minorities became part of the empire. As we'll find if we study the early Christian centuries, the consequence of the close contact between the Roman Empire and the peoples at its borders, especially in the East—contact that impacted administrative and social structures—was that money in the form of metal coins began flowing continuously from the empire out toward the Orient.† In other words, one of the most important events in the first four Christian centuries is that coins streamed out of the empire into the Orient, and this is one of the reasons for the Roman Empire's gradual decline and eventual fall. In the process, the Roman Empire, despite its complex military administration, was getting poorer and poorer in terms of gold and coin.

Of course, this is the outer expression of inner processes, and I'm talking about this outer image of increasing impoverishment in gold and coin only because it is the outer expression or symptom of a soul mood. That soul mood was of great historical significance because something was to develop out of the Roman Empire's growing shortage of precious metals: namely, the individualism that is the outstanding feature of our time. People talked often about the art of making gold, largely because the shortage of gold in Europe awakened a great physical longing for the art of making it. Then the American continent was discovered and gold from there was brought back to Europe. We really must understand these vast contexts and realize that the decline and fall of the Roman Empire affected even alchemy, and thus the development of the human soul—and all of it was due to a shortage of money caused by expanding the empire's social structures beyond the peoples at its borders and into the Orient.

We're now living in times when we have to face the fact that we can no longer live by our instincts alone. We cannot renew our social structures unless we stimulate our thinking about social issues with thoughts based on an understanding of the spiritual world. As it is now, our social sciences are sterile and lifeless, we have maneuvered ourselves into catastrophic times, and all over the world our social structures and institutions are in chaos. All of this could have been prevented if we had allowed spiritual scientific ideas to flow into our development and thinking on social issues, if we had allowed spiritual science to shape the foundations of our society. In other words, there are spiritual causes for the catastrophe of our present time, and the main one is humanity's rebellion against the influence of the spirit. That is in reality what brought about the current catastrophe, for people everywhere rebel against the spirit that wants to work in us.

For example, one way to classify the various worldviews and beliefs is based on external differences; thus, we come up with Catholicism, Protestantism, socialism, naturalism, and so on. Another way to classify them is the one I presented in my talks in Berlin some time ago, namely, on the basis of inner categories, primarily the numbers twelve and seven.[†] Then we'll find there are really seven worldviews: gnosis, logicism, voluntarism, empiricism, mysticism, transcendentalism, and esotericism. Of course, people who merely casually pick up a worldview or two will not use those names. And yet, the music of the spheres prevails everywhere and in everything. Accordingly, even a purely materialistic observer counting the number of worldviews would have to come up with seven of them. He may not call them by their right names, but use names based on how they appear on the outside; still, he'd have to come up with the sum of seven. Indeed, the first article in the current issue of the *Preussische Jahrbücher* (Prussian Yearbooks) offers the results of an attempt to list and classify all worldviews now in existence.† And how many are in his list? Indeed, he lists seven: Catholicism, Protestantism, rationalism, humanism, idealism, socialism, and personal individualism—seven in all. Though these categories are slightly skewed from ours, the sum is inevitably the same, namely, seven. This is an example of how the meaning in our development influences ordinary outer developments and conditions. For the most part people don't want to admit this, but it is of utmost importance for our time to acknowledge this; we must not bury our head in the sand but have the courage to face these facts.

Interesting developments are taking place in our time. In ancient times, in the third post-Atlantean epoch an impulse emanated from the Orient, reached the West, and spread over the whole globe—a radical impulse not derived, as most are today, from material life only, but coming directly from the spiritual realm. Back then, spiritual impulses also influenced how people lived together. Then a certain impulse developed that moved from the East to the West. It manifested in the desire in some people to pass on to others what they had received through many years of experience or through initiation into mysteries, both good and bad. Essentially, they wanted to impose on others what they had acquired. The impulse emanating from the East and moving westward thus was focused on spreading a few spiritual forces among people everywhere for the sake of humanity's progress. The world was to be filled gradually with a few spiritual dictums and forces derived from fading mysteries. All social structures were geared to that goal, and since all this happened in the third post-Atlantean epoch, there are few historical documents or records left of it. However, what is happening now in our time is essentially a recapitulation of what occurred back then. For example, the push from East to West has now, in the fifth post-Atlantean epoch, been transformed into something purely material. In contrast, back then atavistic spiritual powers shaped social structures that would allow humanity to receive strong spiritual impulses that were necessary for our development. In other words, back then humanity was to receive something spiritual. In contrast, now some people want to conquer the material realm of the earth on their own initiative and take it away from others. As a result, so and so many years after the Mystery of Golgotha certain catastrophes occurred. In the process, the Roman Empire fell, and that was the time when spiritual catastrophes befell humanity and certain nations in the East wanted to flood the world with their various dictums. Something very similar is happening now: the Anglo-American people want to take the earth away from all the rest of humankind. That's what's behind the events of our time, and it is a mirror image of what happened in the past—the same except going in the opposite direction. In fact, we cannot really understand what's going on in our time unless we consider humanity's true developmental history, rather than being content with what the history textbooks tell us. More than ever before, it is essential for our future that people become fully aware of what is really happening and find their rightful place within it.

The modern economy has long since been in chaos, and that has led to the current catastrophe. There are two major influences on the situation: first, from West to East the mirror image of what happened in the past, and second, from East to West the stream of outdated and obsolete knowledge and culture. In this latter stream we find vestiges of the ancient spiritual outlook of the Asian Orient, everything people did in those times to spread the spiritual element and integrate it into their lives. A closer look at our current catastrophe will reveal a war of the souls coming from the East, where souls fight for recognition of Oriental and Slavic concepts. At the same time, from West to East a purely material war for markets is raging. To understand these things we must look at them from the perspective of the larger context of humanity's development, and it is important to speak about these things freely. That is, people should be told about what is really happening in the world they live in—it is of the utmost importance to realize the truth. By the same token, we must stop sleeping through what is going on. Currently, people no longer understand even the most important events of our time and can no longer grasp their significance because these things can be understood only in the light of spiritual science; they cannot be comprehended in any other way.

Once we've realized all this, we may wonder what scholars and scientists think of spiritual science these days. A very informative example of this is the book by Oscar Hertwig that I've mentioned before.[†] Hertwig, a student and follower of Ernst Haeckel, wrote an excellent book entitled, *Das Werden der Organismen: Eine Widerlegung der Darwinschen Zufallslehre* (The origin of organisms: a refutation of Darwin's theory of chance), in which he pointed out various flaws in Darwinism, and which I have often praised highly. However, in our spiritual movement we have to abandon blind trust in any kind of authority; accordingly, now that Hertwig has published a second book, you should not assume that just because I praised his previous one, this second one is worth studying too. On the contrary, you'll find this book, entitled *Zur Abwehr des ethischen, sozialen und politischen Darwnismus* (Against Darwinism in ethics, society, and politics), disappointing. While his previous book is excellent, the new one is the worst collection of amateurish and nonsensical things that could possible be said on the topic. Thus, you can't simply go by what I said about the previous book and take it as gospel, for I may have to assign the opposite labels to another book written on the same basis. There's no place here for blind trust in authority; what matters is that you develop your own understanding and insight, your own opinion. The problem in this particular case is that Hertwig is an outstanding natural scientist, but the concepts of the natural sciences cannot be applied to social relationships and structures. If we try to apply them, we find nothing in history but what is already dead or dying, as Gibbon did when he wrote his masterful history of the decline and fall of the Roman Empire.[†]

One of the mysteries of historical development, as I've explained before, is that the concepts of the natural sciences will never lead us to insight into what is growing and unfolding, but only point us to what is decaying or a corpse already. Concepts that work well in the natural sciences are of no use in history except for talking about symptoms of decline. At various times in the past people have sensed this; for example, Treitschke claimed that people's passions and foolish ideas are the real driving forces of history.[†] Of course, that is not true. Rather, unconscious forces descend in the course of historical development, and therefore the obvious way to bring decline into public, and thus practical life is to fill the parliaments with scholars and theorists. The laws these people will make cannot result in anything but symptoms of decline because what is accepted these days in the sciences will only allow us to find such signs of decline in history. It is very important to become aware of this, more important even than most people realize; such awareness is essential if we're honest and sincere about what can bring humanity out of the current catastrophic times. It will no longer do to sleep right through important events that enter our life outside our awareness; events we won't be able to deal with consciously unless we see them in the light of spiritual science. It's a matter of grasping life in its reality and seeing life as it really is. That is why we need to look at how the normal human, the luciferic, and the ahrimanic impulses work together. For we cannot simply decide to be merely normal persons and thus avoid everything luciferic and ahrimanic. Indeed, those who want to be particularly good and upright and to avoid everything luciferic and ahrimanic are most likely to stumble now into the luciferic, now into the ahrimanic sphere. After all, it's not a matter of avoiding those two impulses but of keeping them in balance. Young people in particular have a strong tendency toward the luciferic sphere while adults in their waning years are more drawn toward the ahrimanic. Similarly, women tend more to the luciferic and men more to the ahrimanic impulse, and when we think about the future, our minds are focused on Ahriman's sphere. When we think about the past, looking for what was then only germinating, we're looking into Lucifer's realm. The British Empire belongs to the ahrimanic region while the oriental nations belong to the luciferic. What's important here is to see that these forces are entering our life everywhere; we must not be blind to these things.

For example, in our social structures the luciferic element has at times played a disastrous role because people didn't know how to channel and direct it properly, and allowed that element to get the upper hand and predominate. As a result, the luciferic impulse played an important role in the development of our social structures. Among other things, this led to schools drilling even very young children in competing to be first, second, or at least third. You can imagine the luciferic ambition involved when people want to become the leader or the best in their class. It's the same for all titles, medals, and the like—you can easily see how strongly our social structures are influenced by the luciferic element. And yet, what we must realize is that the time for this kind of ambition is coming to an end. The luciferic element, especially its darker aspects, will gradually wane, at least for the near future, and it behooves us to pay attention to its fading. However, people generally don't notice what is taking the place of the luciferic element, namely, the ahrimanic, which in its own way is just as detrimental. The slogan of the day is now "let ability win through"—but as I've often said, this motto is of little use if people still find their relatives or friends the most able for the job. Clearly, we should not be swayed by abstract slogans but must look at how things are concretely, in reality. However, my point here is that an ahrimanic system with all its dangerous side effects is developing and gaining ground. This system is connected with the attitude embodied in the above-mentioned motto, and in schools it finds expression in so-called aptitude testing, which is widely praised. People talk about all this with such excitement, as if possessed by a demon.

Aptitude tests are to find the most able and gifted students among a certain number—one hundred, let's say—of intelligent boys and girls who are getting good grades. The tests use the most cutting-edge psychological methods to test the students for their intellectual ability, concentration, memory, and so on. For example, experimental psychology has devised a very strange intelligence test in which the children are given three terms—murderer, mirror, rescue—and they have to use their intelligence to find the connection between them. Those who come up with something like, "The murderer sees himself in the mirror, just like everyone else"—well, they're just stupid.

However, those children who find the "most obvious" connection, namely, "A person looks into the mirror, sees the murderer sneaking up on him, and can thus save himself"—now, those are normal. Gifted children, on the other hand, would come up with something like, "The murderer creeps up to the mirror, sees his face in it, is horrified, and decides not to commit the murder." However, the truly and especially gifted ones would say something even cleverer: "There is a mirror near the intended victim, and in the darkness the murderer bumps into the mirror and makes a noise. He then gives up on committing the murder." This is how aptitude tests are done, and they're supposed to be so grand, but are really nothing more than the application of a purely ahrimanic method, which is designed for machines, to human beings. Trying to determine aptitude and giftedness this way will inevitably lead to the most awful effects for our life, in particular, to a growing mechanization of human life.

For a different perspective we need only recall what we used to believe not all that long ago. Then we can easily see that people are talking nonsense when they advocate such tests. For example, many people now considered outstanding and important and admired even by testing enthusiasts—among them the physicist Hermann von Helmholtz—would have been found not gifted and lacking in aptitude if they had been tested in the way I've described.† We must take these things seriously because our future well-being depends on them. We must not be content with empty phrases, but must learn the lessons the events themselves teach us. For example, in the future, say, in the decade from 1930 to 1940, a number of people will be in their forties or early fifties. Now imagine in 1913 you had thought that of the people alive in 1913, a certain number will still be alive in 1930, and some of them will then be in leading positions in society. They will shape our social structures and our outer physical life in many parts of the world. You can imagine what the decade of the 1930s will be like when those who are eighteen or twenty now will be in their forties. Now we have to take into account that many of those people who would have done what we've envisioned happening in the 1930s have died on the battlefields and can no longer be physically involved in managing the affairs of our physical world here. Others will have to take their place. In other words, we can envision two versions of the future and look at them side by side: the future image in which the catastrophe of war had been averted and everything you envisioned in 1913 for the future has come true, and the other future in which many or perhaps all people who could have held leading positions in the 1930s have died on the battlefields in this war. Contemplating these two images will give you a palpable sense of maya, the great illusion of the outer physical plane. After all, the physical world in 1930 will not be the same as it would have been if all those who were young in 1913 had survived. Things would be very different then. It is very important to think about these things, but we can think about them realistically and concretely only with the help of spiritual science. Only with spiritual science can we develop concepts that are no longer bound to our physical brain but go beyond it. Currently, most of our concepts are bound to our physical brain, and that gives a certain characteristic cast to our modern thinking. Because natural scientific concepts, which are especially closely bound to our physical brain, prevail these days, our modern thinking has a special character: it is narrow-minded and parochial. For thinking that is particularly bound to our brain is generally the most narrow-minded. It is up to spiritual science to free our thinking from its bondage to the brain, to get our thoughts moving again. For example, I've presented a number of thoughts to you here today that move nimbly and expand our horizon.

However, not only the horizon of our thoughts but also that of our feelings must be expanded. Sadly, people have become such philistines as a result of their thoughts being closely bound to their physical life. In addition to parochialism, philistinism is a primary trait of our time. Really, most people nowadays think only about what's directly in front of them and are only interested in their own small circle and petty concerns. In contrast, spiritual science will lead us out into the vast expanse of the universe and will unveil to us the larger contexts of events because only on that basis can we understand our present time. Spiritual science must lead us out of philistinism and fight against parochialism and bigotry.

Indeed, even our will has gradually been affected, and as a result of certain social structures that have developed on the basis of our materialistic culture, people have become increasingly clumsy and inept. Clumsiness and awkwardness have taken hold of many. For example, people are sorted into specializations and soon know nothing outside their special area of skill or knowledge; that is, in regard to everything else, they are clumsy, awkward, and inept. Thus, we encounter men nowadays who cannot sew buttons on their pants because they're not tailors by trade. In contrast, spiritual science develops concepts that are alive and enter into our limbs, and thus they make us more adept and skilled. Basically, spiritual science is the antidote to parochialism, philistinism, and ineptness. What we need, now more than ever, is a new age that leads us out of narrow-mindedness, pettiness, and ineptitude toward wider horizons, generosity, and skillfulness. To that end, we must become engaged in spiritual science with heartfelt zeal. Indeed, even the most basic ideas and concepts of spiritual science will show us that the disaster, pain, and suffering of our time—and we have not yet seen the worst of them, not nearly the worst—all this is intimately connected with humanity's rebellion against the spirit. For the most part, we have cut ourselves off from the divine-spiritual life, and now we must regain our relationship to it.

That is what I wanted to emphasize today, so you can increasingly have the feeling that the signs of the times are indeed speaking to us loud and clear, but we will understand them only if we have learned to read them with the help of spiritual science. It is impossible to overstate how seriously and intensively we must study spiritual science; we must continue to permeate our life more and more with what spiritual science gives us. Sadly, people nowadays lack the courage to really think about life and the forces that come to us from the spiritual realm. We must develop this essential courage, otherwise the catastrophe that has befallen humanity will last for a very long time. In other words, spiritual science is a means to find the way out of the conflicts of the present time. I ask you to please take this very seriously and ponder it deeply in your heart; then what we've talked about here today can bear rich fruit in your heart and soul.

6

What Does the Angel Do in Our Astral Body?

ZURICH, OCTOBER 9, 1918

O_{ur} anthroposophical understanding of the spirit is not just a theoretical worldview, but rather an inspiring purpose for our life and a vital force. It is only when we can strengthen the anthroposophical worldview in us so that it comes to life for us that it can truly fulfill its task. Indeed, by uniting our soul with the anthroposophical understanding of the spirit we have, in a sense, become the guardians of certain specific and highly significant processes of humanity's development. Generally, people choosing this or that worldview are convinced that thoughts and ideas only live in their soul but have no other role or existence in the larger context of the world. That is, the adherents of most worldviews believe that their thoughts, ideas, and ideals will become a reality in the world to the extent that people manage to implement them through their physical actions. In contrast, accepting the anthroposophical view means realizing that making our thoughts and ideas come true takes more than just what we can accomplish with our actions in the sensory world. This basic and essential fact already implies that we Anthroposophists are called upon to participate in watching over the signs of the times.

Much is happening in the development of the world, and now, more than ever, it is up to us to develop a true understanding of what is going on in that development in which we also participate.

Everyone knows that to understand an individual we must consider that person's development and not only his or her outer circumstances. For example, the events happening now in the sensory world around us concern us all, whether we are five, ten, twenty, thirty, fifty, or seventy years old. Yet, no reasonable person expects that we will all have the same relationship to the events regardless of our age. To determine how people should relate to their outer environment, we need to consider their individual development, and nobody would doubt this. However, just as the individual undergoes a specific development and has different strengths in childhood, in middle age, and in old age, so humanity as a whole has developed different forces in the course of its development. In a sense, we are sleeping through the world's development if we fail to notice that humanity is essentially different in the twentieth century than it was in the fifteenth or in the time of the Mystery of Golgotha or even before that. It is one of the great failings and troubles of our time that people refuse to consider what I've just pointed out, and believe that they could speak of humanity or of the human being in general and in the abstract without having to take into account that humanity is always developing.

The question then is how we can better understand these things, and we've often talked about important aspects of humanity's development. For instance, we know the Greco-Roman era, which lasted roughly from the eighth century before Christ to the fifteenth century of the Common Era, as the cultural epoch of the intellectual or mind soul; and the period since the fifteenth century is that of the consciousness soul. This alone already tells us something essential about our time in particular, namely, that human development between the fifteenth century and the beginning of the fourth millennium depends primarily on the consciousness soul. However, in spiritual science we must not content ourselves with generalities and abstractions, but must always strive to comprehend concrete facts. Abstractions satisfy at most a very ordinary curiosity, but are otherwise of no use. To make spiritual science come alive for us and be a vital force in our life we must be more serious, rather than merely curious, and must not stop at abstractions such as the ones I've just mentioned. Without a doubt it is true and very important that we're living in the epoch of the consciousness soul and its development, but we must not stop there.

To understand all this more concretely and specifically, we must look more closely at human nature, at what we are like essentially. According to spiritual science, we can distinguish four members of our being. These are, from the top down, the "I," the astral body, the etheric body (which I've recently also called the body of formative forces), and finally the physical body. Of these, the "I" is the one in which we live and are active with our soul and spirit. The "I" is essentially given to us by our development on earth and the spirits of form that direct it, and everything that enters our consciousness comes in by way of the "I." It is the "I" that connects us with the world around us, and if it cannot develop so that it can stay connected—albeit only through the physical body—with the outside world, we will be as unconscious in our waking hours as we are while sleeping. The astral body, on the other hand, is given to us during the Moon evolution that precedes our earthly evolution; the etheric body goes back even further, to the Sun evolution, and the first rudiments of our physical body were formed during the Saturn evolution.

My book *An Outline of Esoteric Science* describes in more detail the complicated processes that led to what we now are as beings composed of the four above-mentioned members.[†] As the facts presented in that book indicate, spirits of various hierarchies have worked together on the three components that envelop our "I": the physical body, etheric body, and astral body, each of which is a very complex structure in itself. Moreover, the hierarchies were not only involved in creating the three spheres around our "I" but are still working in them now. Ultimately, as long as we believe that we are nothing more than an amalgam of bones, blood, flesh, and so on—that is, of elements studied by the ordinary natural sciences; particularly by, physiology, biology, and anatomy—we cannot understand ourselves as human beings. Studying the members of our being more closely will reveal that spiritual beings of the hierarchies are working purposefully and wisely together in the processes that run their course in our body, outside of our awareness. Even the relatively sketchy outline in my above-mentioned *Esoteric Science* shows you already how complicated this collaboration of the various spirits of the higher hierarchies really is. But complicated or not, to understand our being we must study these things closely in concrete detail. To start with, we can ask a concrete yet immensely complicated question, namely, what is the hierarchy of the seraphim or the dynamis, for example, doing now, in 1918, in our etheric body? Indeed, we can ask this kind of question with just as much justification as we can ask whether it is currently raining in Lugano. In both cases, the answer cannot be found by simply thinking or theorizing about the subject; rather, we must get at the facts. For example, we would have to send a telegram or letter to find out whether it's currently raining in Lugano. Similarly, we must delve into the facts to find out, for example, what task the spirits of wisdom or the thrones are currently fulfilling in our etheric body. Of course, such questions are extremely complicated and our answers can only be approximate; this will keep us from becoming proud and arrogant in our striving for true insights and knowledge.

In a sense, the higher beings that concern us directly are the ones about whom we can attain some clarity and certainty; they are also the ones we need to understand clearly so that we're not asleep in regard to their role in our development. We can start with a question that is not as vague and undefined—though it was also quite specific—as the above-mentioned one about the work of the dynamis or thrones in our etheric body. A question to start with, and one that concerns us directly especially in the present time, asks about the work the angels—the higher beings in the hierarchy immediately above us—are currently doing in our astral body. In our inner organization the astral body is directly adjacent to our I, and we thus have every reason to hope that answering the above question will be important to us. Moreover, the angels are the hierarchy directly above ours and are thus, of all hierarchies, the closest to us. Clearly, then, the answer to our modest question about the work of the angels in our astral body at this time in humanity's development, that is, in the twentieth century—in the cultural epoch that began in the fifteenth century and will last until the beginning of the fourth millennium—is of great significance for us. To begin answering such a question, we must take spiritual science seriously; we're not just playing with words and ideas here, but our spiritual science works in areas where the spiritual world becomes accessible. And the hierarchy immediately adjacent to ours can indeed be made palpable and comprehensible.

Not surprisingly, the above-mentioned question can only be answered meaningfully in the epoch of the consciousness soul. You might think that this question could have been asked and even answered in other epochs, but in fact it could not have been answered at all in either the era of atavistic clairvoyance or that of the Greco-Roman culture. Indeed, the images atavistic clairvoyance generated in the soul obscured the activities of the angels in our astral body so that they could not be observed. In other words, those activities could not be seen because of the images generated by atavistic clairvoyance. In the Greco-Roman epoch human thinking was not yet as strongly developed as it is now. Human thinking has undergone a development and become stronger, particularly as a result of the modern scientific age. Consequently, the age of the consciousness soul is the only one in which we can consciously approach questions like the one I mentioned above. As you see, spiritual science does not inundate people with mere theories; rather, it offers concrete insights of far-reaching significance, and in this way proves its usefulness for our life.

To find out what the angels are doing in our astral body, we must advance to a certain level of clairvoyant perception so that we can look into our astral body and see what is going on there. In other words, we have to achieve at least a certain level of imaginative perception if we want to answer the question under discussion. Then we will be able to see that the hierarchy of the angels is forming images in our astral body. The angels are both working jointly and also individually, since each one of them has a specific task to fulfill for the person under his charge—and each of us has an angel, as I've explained before. The angels are forming images in our astral body, and they do so under the direction of the spirits of form. Without imaginative perception we could not know that the angels are continuously forming images in our astral body, images that appear and then vanish again in constant ebb and flow. Without these images we could not develop toward a future that is in line with the intentions of the spirits of form. What the spirits of form want to achieve with us until the end of our earthly development must first be embodied in images, and these images will later be instrumental in transforming humanity; they will then become real. Those are the images the spirits of form are already now creating in our astral body with the help of the angels and reality. We can see and access the images the angels generate in our astral body once we have developed our thinking to a certain level of clairvoyance. We can then observe these images and see that they're formed according to very specific impulses and principles. We'll find that the process that gives rise to these images holds within it the forces for our future development. Strange as this may sound, we can observe the angels as they're working and see that with their work they're carrying out a definite intention for the social structure of our future life on earth. In other words, they want to generate images in our astral body that will lead to specific social conditions and structures for the human society of the future.

Whether we acknowledge the work of the angels for our future or deny it does not matter at all. The angels are working on our ideals for the future regardless. Their work is guided by a specific principle, namely, that in the future nobody shall enjoy happiness in peace as long as there are others who are unhappy. That is, a certain impulse of universal fellowship, of community—fellowship understood in the right way, that is—prevails in regard to social conditions in the physical world. This is one of the impulses according to which the angels form pictures in our astral body. The second impulse that guides the angels' work concerns the intention they have for our soul, our soul life. Regarding this soul life, the angels want to impress images on our astral body that will in the future lead us to see every person we encounter as carrying a spark of the divine concealed within. In other words, the angels are working on changing things. What the angels intend for us is that we no longer consider ourselves merely as higher animals, and solely on the basis of our physical nature. Instead, in our encounters with others, we are to see in everyone a revelation coming from the divine ground of the world, a revelation in flesh and blood. A strong feeling of the divine revelation in every person we meet must animate and guide us at all times. Through their work the angels are preparing us for seeing everyone as an image that reveals itself to us from out of the divine ground of the world, and they embody understanding as seriously, as strongly, and as compassionately as possible in the images they impress on our astral body.

As a result of what the angels intend, in the future people will only become religious on the basis of seeing everyone as an image of God, and this will not be mere theory but permeate their everyday life. This means that in the future there can no longer be a compulsion for people to join a particular religion or denomination—indeed, that will no longer be needed because every encounter with another person will be a religious act, a sacrament. Churches of any kind, and their external institutions in the physical world, will no longer be needed to sustain religious belief. In other words, if the churches understand themselves rightly, they cannot have any other goal but to make themselves redundant on the physical plane by turning all of life into an expression of the supersensory or spiritual realm. In any case, at the bottom of the impulses guiding the work of the angels is the intention to spread religious freedom over all of humanity. In addition, the angels want to enable us to come to the spirit by way of our thinking, to bridge the abyss between the physical world and the spiritual realm with our thinking. In other words: spiritual science for the spirit, religious freedom for the soul, and fellowship for the body—these are the principles resounding like a cosmic melody through the workings of the angels in our astral body. All we need to experience first-hand the angels' wonderful activity in our astral body is to raise our consciousness to a certain higher level.

In summary, we are now living in the age of the consciousness soul, and in this epoch the angels work in our astral body as I've just described. As part of our development, we must gradually come to realize what I've explained. You may wonder where we can find evidence of the angels' work, and at this point we can only find it in the sleeping person. The evidence can be seen in the time between our falling asleep and waking up, as well as in waking sleep states. As I've often pointed out, even when we are awake we often sleep right through our life's most important events. And unfortunately I can assure you that when you look around with open eyes, you will see that these days very many people are really deeply asleep. They don't care about what happens in the world and remain indifferent and detached. The great events of world history often pass them by, just as we don't notice what happens in a city at night while we're sleeping. Though people seem to be awake, in reality they're asleep to what is going on. And it is precisely when people in their waking hours sleep through significant events that we can see how the angels are working in their astral body in the way I've described—and their work is taking place, whether we want to believe it or not.

All this seems mysterious and paradoxical—we often consider this or that person to be unworthy of any kind of relationship to the spiritual world, when in reality the individual in question turns out to be merely quite a sleepyhead in this incarnation, one who sleeps through everything going on around him or her. However, at the same time, the angel is at work in that person's astral body as part of the whole community of angels that is working on the future of humanity. The angel makes use of that individual's astral body regardless, and we can observe the work being done in that astral body. What matters here is that such insights are increasingly pushing their way into our consciousness, and we must therefore develop our consciousness soul to the point of acknowledging what can be discovered only in this way.

Based on these conditions, you will understand that this epoch of the consciousness soul is moving forcefully toward a particular event or change; and because we are dealing with the consciousness soul, it depends on us how this change will play out in our development. Whether sooner or later by a hundred years or so, what will surely occur in our development eventually is that purely by means of our consciousness soul, our conscious thinking, we will learn to see how the angels are preparing our future. In other words, what spiritual science teaches us in this regard must become practical wisdom for our daily life; we must make it our own to such an extent that we can be firmly convinced that the angels work toward the intentions I have outlined above. Since we have already progressed quite far in our development toward freedom, it will depend entirely on us whether we will sleep through the above-described change or move toward it consciously. To move toward this change consciously would mean primarily to study spiritual science; it is offered to us, and all we need to do is study it. In addition, we can support this change by following the suggestions for meditation and other practical directions offered in my book *How to Know Higher Worlds*. Yet, all that is really necessary is to study spiritual science and understand it consciously. You can study spiritual science even without first developing clairvoyance; spiritual science is accessible to anyone who will not put prejudices in his or her way. The more people study spiritual science—the more they make its concepts and ideas their own—the more they will awaken in their consciousness, and not sleep through things but experience them consciously.

Yet, knowing what the angel is doing in our astral body is only the first step; beyond that, the most important thing is to realize that at a certain point three changes will occur. As I said, whether they happen sooner or later will depend on us, and in the worst case those changes will not occur at all. What is supposed to happen is for three insights to be revealed to us through the world of the angels. The first insight is that we can understand the deeper dimensions of our nature with lively, active, human interest. Indeed, there will come a time we don't want to sleep through, a time when we will receive through our angel an inspiring impulse from the spiritual world. That impulse will inspire us to become much more deeply interested in everyone else than we are now. This enhanced interest in our fellow humans will not develop gradually and conveniently, remaining primarily subjective. On the contrary, it will come in one fell swoop when the spiritual world pours into us the mysterious realization of what every person really is. I'm talking about something very concrete and specific here, not some theoretical considerations or reflections, and what I mean is this: people will learn something that makes them interested in everyone else. This is one of the changes I mentioned, and it will immeasurably enrich our social life.

The second revelation from the world of the angels will show us irrefutably that the Christ impulse leads to religious freedom, among other things, and that the hallmark of true Christianity is that it makes absolute freedom of religion possible. The third revelation is the incontrovertible realization that the world is spiritual. As I've explained, this is to occur in such a way that our consciousness soul forms a particular relationship to it, and it is an event that will come at some point in our development because it is what the angel is preparing us for with its images in our astral body. Moreover, the coming event is already embodied in our will. As you know, we can do or fail to do many things, and these days many people still fail to do what can lead us toward an experience of the change indicated, in a fully awake condition. At the same time, there are beings that have an interest in knocking us off track: the ahrimanic and luciferic beings. What I've just explained is part of our divine development. Indeed, if we followed our own spiritual nature, we would have to realize what the angel is unfolding in our astral body. However, the luciferic influence in our development pushes us off course and thus prevents us from realizing the work of the hierarchy of the angels. The luciferic beings push us off track by interfering with our free will and keeping us in the dark about carrying out our free will. Though they make us into good people—indeed, in this context Lucifer wants us to be good and spiritual—they also try to make us into automatons and rob us of our free will. In other words, the luciferic beings want to help become clairvoyant in accordance with the principles of good, but without free will; they want to turn us into clairvoyant automatons, so to speak. By robbing us of our free will, they also take away our ability to choose evil. They want us to act based on spiritual principles, but only as a sort of imitation or copy, without free will. Basically, if the luciferic beings have their way, they will turn us into automatons.

To explain this, we to have take into account certain mysteries of evolution; as you know, the luciferic beings stopped developing at a certain stage in their evolution and now bring alien elements into our otherwise normal development. These luciferic beings are greatly interested in preventing us from fully developing our free will because they themselves have not been able to develop it. Free will can only be attained here on earth, but those beings don't want anything to do with the earth; they are content with having gone through the Saturn, Sun, and Moon evolution; and that's where they want to stop, rather than be part of earthly evolution. Basically, they hate our free will; they act very spiritually but do so automatically—and this is extremely important—and they want to raise us to their level, to their spiritual level. In other words, they want us to be automatons, albeit spiritual ones. The danger there is that if we become spiritual automatons before our consciousness soul is fully functional, we will sleep right through the revelation that is to come, the one I've described above.

The ahrimanic beings are also working to oppose that revelation; they don't want to make us particularly spiritual, but instead aim to deaden our consciousness of our own spirituality. That is, they want to instill in us the belief that we are nothing more than perfectly developed animals. Thus, Ahriman is the great teacher and advocate of materialistic Darwinism, and of those technical and practical activities in our earthly evolution that accept only the outer sensory life as real and deny everything else. Ahriman is behind all endeavors aimed solely at spreading technology for the purpose of more efficiently satisfying our need for food and drink, and our other physical needs that we have in common with the animals. The ahrimanic spirits in our time strive to kill or darken our awareness of being made in the image of God; they want to kill the consciousness soul within us by means of all kinds of sophisticated scientific advances. In previous ages it would not have done any good for the ahrimanic spirits to try to obscure the truth with their theories because during the Greco-Roman epoch—and even more so in still earlier times—people still had atavistic clairvoyance and the pictures it provided, and therefore it didn't much matter what people were thinking. With the help of those inner pictures people could see into the spiritual world, and thus whatever Ahriman might have tried to teach them about their relationship to the animals would not have made any difference in their life. It is really only in our fifth post-Atlantean epoch, which began in the fifteenth century, that thinking has become powerful—we could say it is mighty in its powerlessness. Unlike in previous times, since the fifteenth century thinking has become able to lead the consciousness soul into the spiritual realm, and at the same it also gained the power to prevent that soul from entering the spiritual world. In contrast to earlier eras, in our time theories and sciences are consciously trying to rob us of our divinity and of our experience of the divine. This has not been possible prior to the age of the consciousness soul, and that is why the ahrimanic spirits are trying especially hard now to spread teachings that blot out our awareness of our divine origin.

These explanations of the forces opposing our normal divine development already tell you what you need to do in your life so that you will not be asleep to the revelation that is to come into human evolution. If we're not awake for the coming change, we run the risk that, instead of a significant event that is to intervene powerfully in our future earthly evolution, something detrimental and dangerous to that evolution will take place. Therefore, we must be careful and on the alert. After all, certain spiritual beings advance in their development through ours, that is, they develop right alongside us. For example, the angels that are forming images in our astral body are not doing this just for fun but to accomplish something. What they must accomplish can only be achieved in our earthly development; therefore, if we were to deliberately ignore all this after the development of our consciousness soul, then everything the angel did was for nothing and is reduced to nothing but a game. That is, if we deliberately and consciously ignore what I've talked about here today, the work of the angel is reduced to just a game; it is rendered futile. It is only when we allow these things to become real that the angels' work is redeemed in all its seriousness and purposefulness. This also tells you that the work of the angels must remain serious no matter what—after all, you can imagine the chaos behind the scenes of existence if we could turn the work of the angels into a game merely by being sleepyheads.

You may wonder what will happen if humanity insists on sleeping through the important spiritual revelation that is coming. For example, if people were to sleep through the second part of that revelation, that is, the part about freedom of religion, and thus would miss the recurrence of the Mystery of Golgotha on the etheric plane, then the angels would have to find a different way to do what they had intended to accomplish with the images in our astral body. I've often talked about the coming of the etheric Christ, and if people are not awake for it and for the other simultaneous occurrences, then the angels would have to find another approach. As it turns out, what we don't allow the angels to accomplish by our refusing to wake up to things, they will then have to carry out by means of our sleeping body. In other words, what we are sleeping through in our waking hours and thus prevent the angels from fully accomplishing, those things would then have to be achieved with the help of our sleeping physical body and our etheric body, both of which remain behind in our bed when we're asleep. The angels would then be looking in those bodies for the forces they need to help them accomplish their tasks. The tasks that could not be carried out while we are awake and our waking soul is in our etheric body and physical body will then have to be done with our sleeping etheric body and physical body; that is, during the time when our "I" and our astral body are outside us while we are sleeping.

When we're asleep like this to the important events around us, we run a great risk. That is, if humanity continues with its refusal to turn to the spirit, then at some point before the third millennium the consequences of our stubborn resistance could descend upon us. It's really not long anymore to the third millennium, which begins in the year 2000. If the angels have to work with our sleeping body instead of being able to use our waking soul to accomplish their task, they would have to move all their work out of our astral body and immerse it in our etheric body in order to carry out their mission. However, we will not be there and thus not be part of this. If the angels have to carry out their task in the etheric body, they can do so only if we're not there, because if we were there in our waking state, we would keep the angels from doing their work. This gives you a general picture of the risk involved in not wanting to be awake to things.

In particular, if the angels had to do their work in our etheric body and our physical body while we're sleeping—that is, they would have to work in our absence—three things will occur in humanity's development. First of all, as the angels work in our sleeping body, in the absence of our astral body and "I," a certain instinctive power will be created, and we will simply find it there when we wake up in the morning. In other words, we'll simply be given certain instinctive insights rather than having to attain them through our freedom;

what we find as we wake up every morning will be instinct rather than being based on our free consciousness. These instinctive insights are indeed part of our development and are connected to the mysteries of conception and birth, to our whole sexual life. They become dangerous and harmful when we receive them as a result of the above-described refusal to wake up to the angels' work in our astral body. If these angels then have to work in our etheric body, in our absence, they themselves will undergo a certain change that I cannot talk about because it is one of the higher secrets of initiation science that must not yet be revealed. However, what I can tell you is that if human development takes the turn described above, then certain sexual instincts will emerge and gain ground, not in a beneficial or useful way in our waking, clear consciousness, but in a destructive way as pure instincts. These instincts will not only sidetrack us but will also influence our social structures; in particular, what will then enter our bloodstream as a result of our sexual life will keep us from developing any kind of fellowship on earth. Instead, these instincts would goad us at all times into rebelling against fellowship, a rebellion that would be purely instinctual.

Thus, we face a moment of decision, a decisive crossroads: either we go to the right, and then we must be awake to things, or we got to the left, and then we can sleep through everything. However, in this latter case, instincts will emerge that will have dreadful consequences. Natural scientists' response to the emergence of these instincts will be to say that this development was inevitable and an absolute necessity, that it is simply inherent in human evolution. That is why the natural sciences cannot warn us about such things or tell us much about them. After all, whether human beings turn into angels or devils, the natural sciences would have an explanation in either case, for to them everything happens as a result of what precedes it. There you have the great wisdom of explanation based on causality. The natural sciences will not even notice the event I've described here today because they will naturally consider it an absolute necessity that people become near-devils because of their sexual instincts. Basically, we cannot explain these things by means of the natural sciences because for them everything can be explained scientifically.

It is only through spiritual, supersensible insight that these things can be understood.

The second consequence that will follow from the work that will cause changes in the angels is an instinctive but detrimental knowledge of certain remedies. Indeed, everything related to medicine will get a tremendous boost in the materialistic sense. People will instinctively perceive the healing properties of certain substances and certain activities and will do great harm with that, but they will call the harm they do useful and beneficial. As a result, people will call the sick healthy, for they will realize that then they can get involved in certain activities, perform certain actions, that they will enjoy. Indeed, people will enjoy doing what is unwholesome. Basically, there will be growing knowledge of the healing properties of certain processes and activities, but it will lead us onto dangerous ground. Above all, people will learn through certain of their instincts which illnesses are caused by certain substances and actions, and then they can decide, on the basis of purely egotistic motives, whether to produce these illnesses or not.

The third consequence of the above-described turn in human development will be that we come to know certain forces that can easily be manipulated to unleash vast mechanical power over the whole world. Simply harmonizing certain vibrations can release tremendous powers. As a result, we will be able to instinctively exert some control over the realm of mechanics and machines, and then technology as a whole will be on dangerous ground. Our egotism will be pleased with this development and find it useful. To properly appreciate these concrete details concerning our development, we must develop a spiritual view of life. For without it, if we rely on an unspiritual view, these things will remain unclear to us. Without a spiritual view of life, we would be at a loss when the above-described harmful medicine takes hold, when our sexual instincts go badly astray, when the world mechanism goes awry regarding the use of natural resources through spiritual powers. Without a spiritual worldview, we would not be able to understand or even notice these things and how they are pushing us off our true path. Indeed, without spiritual understanding we would be much like the sleeping person who does not notice the thief coming at night to rob him and only sees the damage later, when waking up, and by then it is too late.

It would be a rough awakening indeed: we would delight in the expansion of our instinctive knowledge of the healing properties of certain substances and processes, we would enjoy living out our sexual instincts gone awry, and we would praise particularly this last aberration as an exceptionally fine form of the superhuman and of impartiality and tolerance. In a sense, what is ugly would become beautiful for us and vice versa, and we would not even notice this because it would appear to us as an absolute necessity—as the way things must be. Nevertheless, we would be off our true course, which has been prescribed for us even in regard to our own inner nature. In contrast, once we accept spiritual science and develop a sense for how it can color our outlook on everything, we can seriously consider the truths I've talked about here today. Then we can draw from these truths what we can also draw from spiritual science as a whole: namely, that spiritual science also implies a certain commitment, a lifetime commitment. Regardless of what we're doing or where we are, the important thing is always to remember that everything we do must be steeped in and illuminated by our anthroposophical consciousness. And that is how we can contribute to advancing the development of humanity in the right way. Indeed, it is a grave mistake to believe that spiritual science, understood rightly and sincerely, would ever lead us away from the practical and important work of our life. True spiritual science awakens us to the things I've talked about today, and the question then is whether our waking life can ever be bad for our sleep. We can use an analogy here and say that insight into the spiritual world is to our normal waking state like a further waking up, just as our normal waking state is an awakening from sleep. Our question then is whether this waking life can ever interfere with our sleep. Of course, our sleep will suffer if we lead an irregular, disorderly life. If we live a wholesome, orderly life while we're awake, then we'll sleep well and wake up rested and refreshed. However, if we spend our waking hours daydreaming, snoozing off, idly lounging about rather than working, then we won't sleep well. The same applies to the waking life we attain through spiritual science; if we use spiritual science to develop a solid and orderly relationship to the spiritual world, then this right relationship will get us on the right track in our ordinary sensory life here in the physical world.

If we're at all awake these days, we cannot fail to notice that, especially in recent decades, people often boast of their so-called practical experience in life. Indeed, these days those who have the greatest disdain for ideals and everything spiritual have managed to get into leadership positions all over the world. They could proclaim all they wanted about this practical experience as long as humanity did not get dragged into the abyss with them. However, now some of them are starting to groan—instinctively, for the most part—and call for a new era to begin and for new ideals. But it's just instinctive groaning, and if these things were to come about without people consciously delving into spiritual science, they would be more conducive to the deterioration of what we are to experience in our waking state, rather than to any kind of beneficial advance in our development. Nowadays those who speechify and trot out the old saws may still meet with applause, but people will have to get used to hearing other words, other ideas, if a social cosmos is to arise out of the current chaos.

The truth is that if we fail to be awake when we should be and thus do not discover what should be happening, then nothing real can happen. Instead, the ghost of the preceding epoch will haunt us, much as many religious denominations of our time are haunted by the ghosts of the past and as our laws are haunted by those of ancient Rome. Particularly in this regard, the mission of spiritual science in the age of the consciousness soul is to set us free by leading us to the true observation of a spiritual fact, namely, the work of the angel in our astral body. Talking abstractly about angels and so on can at best be the first step; true progress can be made only if we speak concretely, that is, if we answer the most burning question that concerns us in relation to our specific time. The question we've talked about here today concerns us deeply because the angel weaves images in our astral body that are to give a certain form to our future, a form that is to be implemented by the consciousness soul. If we did not have a consciousness soul, we would not have to concern ourselves with these things; in that case, other spirits and other hierarchies would intervene to accomplish what the angel is weaving in our astral body. However, since we are to develop our consciousness soul, no other spirits can step in to take the place of the angel and carry out what the angel is weaving.

Of course, the angels were also at work in the human astral body in the ancient Egyptian period, but very soon other spirits stepped in and as a result people's atavistic-clairvoyant consciousness was obscured. In other words, thanks to their atavistic clairvoyance people could see the angels' activity and therefore wove a thick dark veil to cover the work of the angels. However, now, in our time, our task is to unveil the angels' activity, and that is why we should not sleep through what will be carried into our conscious life in our age, which will end before the third millennium. Anthroposophical spiritual science therefore wants to give us not just teachings and insights but above all intentions, intentions that will give us the strength to be awake.† Indeed, we can make it a habit to be awake if we become more attentive. To begin with, if we pay attention, we find that not a day goes by that a miracle doesn't happen in our life. We can turn this around and say that if on any day we don't find a miracle in our life, it's only because we have lost sight of it. Simply review your day in the evening, and you'll find some event—whether small or big or medium-sized—of which you have to say that it was a strange thing to have happened, and that it has come into your life in a peculiar way. You'll see this clearly if you just widen the horizon of your thinking and consider your life in a sufficiently comprehensive context. Of course, people generally don't do this because they usually don't ask themselves what events were prevented from occurring simply because something else took place.

By and large, we don't concern ourselves with the events that did not happen but were prevented and that would have changed our life radically if they had occurred. Yet, what is behind those events that are in this way kept out of our life can teach us to be awake and alert. For example, as we review our day in the evening, we could ask what could have happened to us that day. When we look at this or that event and think about what consequences it could have had, the reflections this evokes can then teach us to be awake and disciplined.

This is just a beginning, but from there we can progress almost effortlessly further and further. Finally, we will begin to think more deeply about the significance of events for our life. For example, if we had planned to go out at 10:30 in the morning but are delayed because someone drops by for a visit at the last minute, we may be annoyed at the delay but will then also think about what might have happened if we had left the house as planned. We will then consider what changes have been wrought in our life as a result of our not leaving on time.

I've talked about these things here previously in greater detail. A straight path leads from the perception of the negative in our life, which can nevertheless testify to the wise guidance of our life, all the way to the perception of the angel working and weaving in our astral body; it is a straight, safe, and clear path that we can easily follow. We'll talk more about this a week from today in the second lecture to be offered here.

7

How Can I Find Christ?

Today we'll continue the reflections we began last week about the role our soul must play in the spiritual world in the future and how to prepare for this. In particular, I'd like to talk in more detail about how we must experience the Christ mystery after we've prepared ourselves for that through the spiritual ideals I've mentioned last time. To begin with a general statement that will be explained in detail later on: seen from the vantage point of spiritual science, with the methods spiritual science provides, our soul is connected, on the one hand, to our physical body and, on the other, to our spiritual life, and there are essentially three things in our soul that move us toward the spiritual world, three desires or urges, we might say. We would have to deny these three urges inherent in our soul if we want to refuse to learn anything about the spiritual world. At any rate, first of all, we have an inner urge to know the divine (to use a general term). Second, we have the desire to know Christ—of course, we're talking here about human beings in the current period of development. And third, we have the urge to come to know what is generally called spirit or Holy Spirit. As you know, some people deny that we have these three tendencies, and especially in the nineteenth century, we have seen to what extremes people all over Europe will go in their outright rejection of the divine.

In spiritual science, of course, we do not doubt the divine or the spiritual realm in which we can say the divine resides. Based on that perspective and conviction, then, we can ask why people deny what in the Trinity we call God the Father. Spiritual science reveals that people who deny God the Father—that is, the divine as such as well as the divine as it was revered in the Israelite religion—suffer from a real physical defect, a physical illness, or physical deficiency; they suffer from a problem in the physical body. In other words, according to spiritual science, to be an atheist means to have some kind of illness, one that physicians cannot cure, of course. Indeed, physicians are often suffering from the same affliction, one that is not yet recognized by modern medicine as an illness. Nevertheless, spiritual science finds this disease present in all those who deny what they must feel in our time, not through the constitution of their soul but through that of their physical body. When people deny what a healthy and wholesome feeling in their body tells them is true—namely, that a divine element permeates the world—they become physically ill according to the spiritual-scientific definition of illness.

In addition, very many people deny Christ, and spiritual science considers this denial a matter of destiny that concerns our soul life. According to spiritual science, denying Christ is a misfortune; to deny God is to be ill, but to deny Christ is to be unfortunate indeed. Whether we can find our way to Christ is in a sense a matter of destiny, and influences our individual karma. It is a misfortune not to have a relationship to Christ. On the other hand, denying the Holy Spirit signals a certain stupor of one's own spirit. We are made of body, soul, and spirit, and we can have disorders or deficiencies in any one or all three of them. There is a real physical pathological deficiency present in atheists. Failing to find in this life a connection to the world where the Christ is revealed is a true misfortune. Inability to find the spirit inside oneself is a kind of stupor, a sort of subtle idiocy, which is not yet recognized by the medical establishment.

The question to consider, then, is how we can find our way to Christ, and that is our topic for today: how we can find Christ in the course of our life through our own soul. The question of how to find Christ is often asked by seriously searching souls, but to answer it meaningfully requires considering it in a certain historical context. We'll now look at that historical context that will lead us in the course of our reflections today to discover an answer to that question of how to find Christ. As you know, from the perspective of spiritual science, our current historical epoch began in the fifteenth century, approximately in 1413. But if we don't want to get confused by numbers, we can simply say that in the fifteenth century human soul life became what it still is today. Modern historians generally don't want to accept this because they're only looking at outer facts and have no idea that before the fifteenth century people were thinking and feeling quite differently and acted out very different impulses; they were radically different from what we are now in our soul life. History as it is presented in modern textbooks is merely a convenient fabrication, a fiction, and therefore historians have no understanding of what we're talking about here. The epoch that came to an end in 1413 had begun in 747 B.C.E., that is, in the eighth century before Christ. Accordingly, in spiritual science we consider the Greco-Roman cultural epoch to have lasted from 747 B.C.E. until 1413. As you know, this is the epoch when the Mystery of Golgotha took place—roughly in the first third of that period. For centuries the Mystery of Golgotha was the pivotal point in the life of many people, in their thinking and feeling. In fact, human souls grasped the Mystery of Golgotha in a particularly emotional and intense way in the period preceding our modern time, that is, before the fifteenth century. This was followed by the period in which the gospels were widely read in all segments of the population. This was also the time when the debates about the historical authenticity and accuracy of the gospels began. And as you know, those disputes have continued to our day and have been carried to extremes. Though these arguments play a big role, especially among protestant theologians, we will not discuss its various developments in detail but merely consider what can be said today about what people intend with this quarrel about the Mystery of Golgotha.

In our materialistic age people insist on having material proof for everything. In the discipline of history, the term "proven" refers to anything that can be substantiated with documents. When historians come across records, they assume that the events recorded in those documents actually happened. Most likely, the gospels cannot be said to be that conclusive. As you know from my book *Christianity as Mystical Fact*, the gospels are certainly not historical documents or records; rather, they are books of inspiration and initiation.† In the past they have often been taken as historical records, but through careful research people have found out that they are definitely not historical records. It has also been found that all the other parts of the Bible are not historical records either. And Adolf Harnack, who is a renowned theologian—though unjustly so—has done more research on the Bible and found that everything we can historically verify about the person of Jesus Christ fits on one quarto page, as he put it.† Strange as it may sound, the only part of that statement that is correct is that even what we might write on that quarto page is actually not true and cannot be proven historically. What is true is only that there are no tenable historical records about the Mystery of Golgotha. From the perspective of modern historical research, we have to admit that there is no outer evidence for the Mystery of Golgotha—and for good reason.

Divine wisdom decreed that the Mystery of Golgotha should not be provable by external materialistic means for the simple reason that this most important event in the history of the earth should be understandable only spiritually, in a supersensory way. Those looking for outer materialistic evidence will not find any, but because of their criticism they'll only find out that there is no evidence. In other words, the Mystery of Golgotha forces us to make a decision: either we resort to the spiritual realm, or we cannot understand the Mystery of Golgotha at all. In a sense, then, the Mystery of Golgotha is to force our soul to turn away from any sensory proof and toward the spiritual realm. Thus, there is a good reason why there is no scientific or any other historical evidence for the Mystery of Golgotha. Indeed, the important contribution of spiritual science will be to lead people to a spiritual understanding of the Mystery of Golgotha in the way I've describe many times before. Spiritual science will come into its own in this connection when all external sciences that are based exclusively on the sensory realm will have to admit that the Mystery of Golgotha is no longer accessible to it, when even critical theology begins to act in an unchristian way, and only the spiritual path to the Mystery of Golgotha is left.

You may wonder what the situation of humanity was like at the time when the Mystery of Golgotha occurred during the fourth post-Atlantean epoch in the Greco-Roman cultural period. Well, you already know the significance of that period, and you know that humanity undergoes a development throughout history that recapitulates the evolution of the various members of the human being. As you know, in the Egypto-Chaldean cultural period, which preceded the year 747 B.C.E., human beings developed what we call their sentient soul; in the Greco-Roman cultural period they developed their intellectual or mind soul; and ever since the year 1413 in our fifth post-Atlantean epoch we've been developing our consciousness soul. In other words, the Greco-Roman cultural period between 747 B.C.E. and 1413 was primarily the period for educating humanity—to speak with Lessing here—in how to use the intellectual or mind soul in freedom.† In the middle of that time period—that is, the point at which the ascending line of development of the consciousness soul becomes a descending one—this midpoint, as you can easily figure out yourself, occurred in the year 333 after the birth of Christ. Clearly, then, the year 333, the midpoint of the Greco-Roman cultural period, is a very important year in human development. And exactly 333 years earlier the event that led to the Mystery of Golgotha occurred, namely, the birth of Christ. To fully appreciate the situation of humanity, we must reflect on what would have happened if the Mystery of Golgotha had not occurred. We can properly appreciate the significance of the Mystery of Golgotha when we consider what would have happened if that event had not taken place. Obviously, if it had not happened, humanity would have reached the middle of the fourth post-Atlantean epoch, the year 333, only by virtue of its own elementary powers. Humanity would have had to develop out of itself all the capacities belonging to the intellectual or mind soul, so that we would have had them available in the following centuries.

This developmental trajectory was radically changed through the occurrence of the Mystery of Golgotha—that is, something very different happened on account of that event, something tremendously different from what would have taken place without it. Taking a closer look at the Mystery of Golgotha, we see that it is the central and special event that gives meaning to the whole earth, and its most important characteristic is that we can only understand it through a transcendental approach, a spiritual approach. There is no other way to the Mystery of Golgotha except a spiritual one. You may wonder why this is the case. Well, the reason for this is that, although around the year 333 in the fourth post-Atlantean epoch people were approaching the full flowering of their intellectual or mind soul, in their physical life between birth and death they were very far from being able to understand the true nature of the Mystery of Golgotha with their ordinary human capacities. In other words, no matter how old we get or how much we mature and learn, the capacities we develop as a result of our physical development between birth and death will not enable us to understand the Mystery of Golgotha. That is also the reason why Christ's contemporaries, even those who loved Jesus, such as the apostles, could understand what they were supposed to understand, namely, who Christ Jesus really was, only because they had a certain kind of atavistic clairvoyance. It was through that atavistic clairvoyance that they had any idea at all of who was living in their midst; their own human capacities would not have been sufficient to make this understanding possible. Moreover, they wrote the gospels with the help of ancient mystery books. Thus, they wrote the mighty gospels based on their ancient atavistic clairvoyance, not on the basis of the natural human capacities they had developed by that time.

However, our soul continues to develop even after it has crossed the threshold of death and in the process its powers of understanding grow; and thus, even after death, the soul comes to understand more and more. Interestingly, out of their love for Christ, the apostles had prepared themselves for living in Christ after death, and they were only able to fully understand the Mystery of Golgotha with their own human capacities three hundred years later. In other words, the apostles and disciples who lived with Christ entered the spiritual world after their physical death, and in that world their capacities and powers continued to grow much as they do here in the course of our physical life. This means that at the moment of death our understanding is not as developed as it will be two hundred years later. It wasn't until almost three hundred years after the event that Christ's contemporaries were able to understanding out of their own powers what they had seen here on earth. That is, it was only after two or three hundred years of further development in the spiritual realm, where we dwell between death and rebirth, that they could understand this event they had seen firsthand in their life on earth. And once they had come to such an understanding, they began to inspire people living here on earth.

In fact, the second- and third-century writings of the so-called fathers of the church must be read in this light; we understand what they wrote about Christ Jesus when we realize who inspired them. The inspiration from the dead contemporaries of Christ Jesus was written down by the church fathers in the third century. The church fathers had a strange way of expressing themselves in their writing about Christ Jesus, one that people nowadays—and we'll talk more about them shortly—find nearly impossible to understand. For example, our modern materialistic culture heaps disdain on one of them in particular, namely, on Tertullian, because he is supposed to be the author of a statement that is anathema to this culture.[†] Tertullian said, "*Credo quia absurdum est*," that is, "I believe what is foolish and not what is reasonable."[†] Tertullian lived at the time when Christ's dead disciples in the spiritual world began inspiring people here on earth, and he was one of the people so inspired. Like everyone else, Tertullian wrote in accordance with his individual constitution and style; after all, whatever inspirations may come, we always receive them in our own individual way. Thus, Tertullian passed on the inspirations he had received not in a pure and unadulterated fashion, but refracted by his ability to express himself and his natural human limitations: first, he lived in a mortal body, and second, he was in a certain way very passionate and even fanatic. Thus, he wrote as was natural and typical for him, and his writings now seem very strange to us when we consider them rightly.

As proper study will show, Tertullian, a Roman citizen, was a very eloquent and moving writer even though he did not have much of a literary education. Indeed, in a sense, it was Tertullian who made

Latin a language fit for Christianity. He was the one who found a way
to make Latin—which is really the most prosaic and purely rhetorical
language—glow with spirit and holy passion; and that's why we find
a true living soul in his works, especially in his *De carne Christi* (On
the Flesh of Christ) and in the book in which he refutes all the accu-
sations brought against the Christians back then. These works are
written with great, holy passion and magnificent eloquence. As can be
seen from his *De carne Christi*, though a Roman himself, Tertullian
was nevertheless impartial regarding Rome and the Romans. He
passionately defended the Christians against persecution by the
Romans; he fervently condemned the Romans for torturing the
Christians to make them deny their faith in Christ Jesus, and went
so far as to say that their actions in judging the Christians more than
sufficiently prove the Romans' injustice. Basically, Tertullian told
the Romans, "you must change your usual judicial process and not
apply it when you're dealing with Christians. In all other cases, you
use torture to force witnesses to tell the truth, to confess what they
really think and to stop telling lies. In contrast, when you're torturing
Christians, you want them to deny what they really believe. That is,
as judges you act toward the Christians in the opposite way as you do
when judging others. In all other cases, you use torture to find out
the truth, but in the case of the Christians you do it to hear them tell
a lie." In a nutshell, this is what Tertullian said to the Romans, and
his words really hit the nail on the head.

Tertullian's writings reveal him as a courageous, determined man
who realized how idolatrous and empty the Romans' worship of
their gods really was, and openly denounced it. At the same time,
he showed himself in all his writings as having a close relationship to
the spiritual world. For example, he wrote about demons as though
they were his personal acquaintances. Among other things, Tertullian
challenged his readers to ask the demons whether Christ really is the
true God, as the Christians claim. As Tertullian put it, "Put a true
Christian next to a person possessed by a demon, and when you get
the demon to talk, you'll find that he admits being a demon because
he cannot help telling the truth." Indeed, as Tertullian knew, demons
always tell the truth when they're asked a question and never lie in

response. Tertullian concluded from this, "Thus, the demons will also tell you the truth, and when the Christian asks them sincerely whether Christ Jesus is the true God, they demons will answer that he is indeed the true God. Of course, the demons hate and fight against Christ, but they will still tell you that he is the true God." In other words, Tertullian based his argument not on the testimony of other people but on that of demons. According to him, demons are witnesses that aren't just saying what we want to hear but that truly confess that Christ is God. That is what Tertullian discovered for himself.

Clearly, reading Tertullian, who was so obviously under the influence of the above-described inspiration, one can't help wondering what he himself believed in the depths of his soul. Indeed, we can learn much from Tertullian's deepest beliefs because he already sensed what was not revealed to people until long after his own death. Basically, Tertullian believed, first, that human beings at his time (that is, in the late second century C.E.) were so constituted as to be subject to the shame and disgrace of denying the greatest event in the history of the world, an event they could never come to on their own. Second, Tertullian believed that the human soul was too weak to understand this pivotal event; and third, he believed that if people follow only what their mortal body makes them capable of, they will find it impossible to establish a relationship to the Mystery of Golgotha. These three things are at the core of what Tertullian believed, and on that basis he once said, "The Son of God was crucified; I am not ashamed because men must need be ashamed of it. And the Son of God died; it is by all means to be believed, because it is absurd."† His words are, "*Prorsus credibile est, quia ineptum est,*" meaning that it is credible precisely because it is absurd or foolish. Tertullian is imputed to have said "*Credo, quia absurdum est,*" but this sentence does not appear anywhere in Tertullian's work or in the work of any other church father; the previous sentence, however, does appear in Tertullian's book. Unfortunately, the misquoted sentence is all most people know about Tertullian and his work. The third important thing he said is, "And He was buried, and rose again; the fact is certain, because it is impossible"—we must believe it precisely because it is impossible.†

As you can imagine, these three statements of Tertullian appear particularly appalling to people in our modern and clever times. You can imagine the reaction of your typical dyed-in-the-wool educated materialist to the notion that Christ was crucified and we must believe it because it is humiliating and shameful; Christ died, and we must believe it because it is absurd; Christ was truly raised from the dead, and we must believe it because it is impossible. Well, you can easily see what people with a monist worldview would have to say to that. Now, thanks to the inspiration he received, Tertullian was an unusually keen judge of human nature for his time. He realized what path humanity was pursuing in his time. In his time humanity was living through the Greco-Roman cultural period in the fourth post-Atlantean epoch and moving toward the future. Now, at a point as many years in the future as the Mystery of Golgotha was in the past, certain spiritual powers had intended to guide earthly development in a direction very different from the one it took as a result of the occurrence of the Mystery of Golgotha. That is, Tertullian's time, the year 333—the point exactly 333 years after the Mystery of Golgotha—was the midpoint, and the new direction in earthly development was planned for 333 years after that, namely, for the year 666. This is the year the writer of the Book of Revelation speaks of so passionately, and I recommend that you read those passages about the year 666.[†] Certain spiritual powers had intended for certain things to happen to humanity in that year, things that would have happened if the Mystery of Golgotha had not taken place. Those powers wanted to use the descending line of development of the intellectual or mind soul that began in 333, the year that this development reached its peak, to steer humanity onto a very different track from the one the divine beings connected with us since the beginning, since the Saturn evolution, had intended for us.

Essentially, what those powers intended was to give us through a kind of revelation already in 666 what was otherwise not to enter our development until later, namely, the consciousness soul and its contents. If those powers, beings opposed to our evolution but who want to usurp and rule it, had been able to carry out their intentions, humanity would have been as surprised in 666 by suddenly having a consciousness soul as it will be long after we're gone. This is typical of what those beings who love humanity but hate the gods always do: they want to move to an earlier time all those things planned for us by the spiritual beings who have our best interests at heart; the latter intend for those things to happen in their due course, when humanity is ready for them, rather than prematurely. In this case, what is planned for the middle of our epoch—that is, for 1080 years after the year 1413, namely, the year 2493—would have been injected into humanity by ahrimanic-luciferic powers already as early as 666. However, human beings will not be ready until 2493 where the conscious comprehension of their own personality is concerned. Those ahrimanic-luciferic powers wanted to give us our consciousness soul at that earlier time, but in the process they would have changed our nature so that it would be impossible for us to find the way to the spirit self, life spirit, and spirit human. That is, they would have cut off our path to the future and taken us over for a very different kind of development.

Fortunately, none of that happened in the grand and devilish way it was planned, but traces of it can still be found in history because certain things happened that, though carried out by people, were actually instigated by certain spiritual beings; that is, people merely acted as puppets and the spiritual beings pulled the strings. For example, the emperor Justinian was one such puppet of those beings, and acted under their influence and direction when he closed the schools of philosophy in Athens in 529.† Justinian was a fervent enemy of ancient Greek wisdom and everything connected with it, and by shutting down the schools he expelled the last remnants of Greek learning and Aristotelian-Platonic philosophy, and forced scholars and philosophers to flee to Persia. Earlier, in the fifth century, Zeno Isauricus had already expelled other Greek sages from Edessa, and they and Syrian scholars had fled to Nibisi. And there, in Persia, as the year 666 approached, the representatives of the most exquisite and outstanding learning gathered at the Academy of Gondishapur.† Most of them had come from Greece and had ignored the Mystery of Golgotha. The faculty at the Academy of Gondishapur was inspired by luciferic-ahrimanic powers. The development that those powers had wanted to occur in 666, namely, the introduction of the consciousness soul at that early point, and the consequent cutting off of our future development, was supported by the Academy of Gondishapur. If that development had occurred, then extremely learned and exceptionally brilliant people would have appeared in various places in the course of the seventh century; and their mission would have been to spread in their wanderings the culture of 666 as it had been planned by the Academy of Gondishapur, all over Western Asia, North Africa, Southern Europe, and eventually all of Europe. This culture would have directed people's attention, already back then, exclusively to their own personality, their consciousness soul.

It was not possible for this to occur because the world had already taken on a different form and no longer provided the ground on which such events could have developed. As a result, the jolt the Academy of Gondishapur was to give Western culture was blunted. Instead of producing the kind of wisdom compared to which our current outer knowledge is a mere trifle and spiritually revealing the wisdom about everything we will gradually discover through experiments and the natural sciences up to the year 2493, we only have the vestiges of all this in what Arab scholars brought with them to Spain. That is, instead of brilliant and magnificent learning, we only have remnants of past great wisdom—and these remnants are only blunted and not as vivid as was intended—and also Islam, the teachings of Muhammad.† In other words, Islam has taken the place of what should have come from the Academy of Gondishapur. Ultimately, through the Mystery of Golgotha the world was steered away from that detrimental development. This redirection is due to the earlier occurrence of the Mystery of Golgotha, and also to the fact that it is an event that cannot be understood with the usual human capacities that we develop between birth and death. As a result, the development I described above occurred in Western cultures, namely, the inspiration coming from the dead, which we've seen in Tertullian. This inspiration turned people's attention to the Mystery of Golgotha and thus to something very different from the influences that would have come from the Academy of Gondishapur. Thanks to these developments, a grand but devilish wisdom, which was cultivated by the Academy of Gondishapur, could not get a foothold;

but at the same time, the spread of that wisdom for the benefit of humanity was also prevented. Much of the inspiration coming from the dead was passed on by people only in fragmentary, incomplete, or refracted form, but it still saved humanity from undergoing what would have happened, what would have entered the human soul, if the Academy of Gondishapur had been successful in carrying out its plan.

Events such as the ones planned by the Academy of Gondishapur take place behind the scenes of the world's outer development, in the spiritual realm. Though they have a connection to such events, they take place in the spiritual realm, and therefore we cannot really judge them—neither the events intended by the Academy of Gondishapur nor the Mystery of Golgotha—solely on the basis of what happens in the physical world. To fully understand such events we must look much, much deeper than people usually think. As I've explained, there are indeed traces in the world of what should have happened but was blunted, so that instead of something grand and brilliant we now have Islam. Clearly, something did happen to humanity; in particular, the impulse of Gondishapur, the neo-Persian impulse, reintroduced the Zarathustra impulse anachronistically, at the inappropriate time. And as a result, humanity as a whole suffered a sort of inner breakdown—if I may put it like this—that has had an impact on our physical body. The impulse people received back then affected their body, and to this day we are born with that same effect. This impulse is really the above-mentioned sickness people have been infected with, and its expression is the denial of God the Father.

Please don't misunderstand me: modern civilized people everywhere have a thorn in their flesh, so to speak. As you know, St. Paul had much to say about that thorn in the flesh, including many prophecies.[†] He was an especially advanced person for his time and therefore already had that thorn in his flesh, but the rest of humanity has had it only since the seventh century. This thorn will spread more and more and become ever more important. For example, people who succumb fully to this thorn, this sickness—for it is really a thorn in the physical body, an illness—will become atheists; they will deny God and the divine realm. In modern civilizations, everyone has a predisposition to atheism; it's only a matter of whether we give in to it or not. In other words, we all have within us the illness that can goad us into denying the divine, even though our true nature would lead us to acknowledge it. In a sense, our nature became slightly mineralized in the past, it regressed in its development, and as a result we all carry the disease of God denial, of atheism, in us. This disease has a number of effects; among other things, it creates a stronger bond of attraction between our soul and our physical body, a bond that is stronger than in previous times and also stronger than what our true nature calls for. In a sense, a strong bond is forged between soul and body, and although the soul, by virtue of its own nature, is not intended to take part in the body's destiny, this bond joins its fate more and more to that of the body, even in the moments of birth and death.

What the sages at the Academy of Gondishapur wanted to achieve—and what in a more amateurish way secret societies in our time also want—is nothing less than to make people very wise for life on earth. Their plan was to do this by inculcating people's souls with this wisdom and thus letting the soul have a part in death. After passing through the portal of death, these souls would then not have been inclined to participate in spiritual life or their subsequent incarnations. In other words, the intention was to cut off our future development. The beings connected with the Academy of Gondishapur wanted to seize humanity for themselves and for a very different world; they wanted to tear us out of our earthly development, to keep us from fulfilling our mission here of learning and developing slowly and gradually so that we can eventually come to the spirit self, life spirit, and spirit human. If those beings had had their way, our soul would have come closer to the earth than it was supposed to. Dying, which is the body's destiny, would also have become that of the soul. This was prevented from happening by the Mystery of Golgotha; that event released us from the close relationship to death that was about to be forged. To counterbalance the closer bond between soul and body that had been forged by a certain stream in world evolution, Christ bound the soul more closely to the spirit than had originally been intended. Thus, the Mystery of Golgotha linked the soul more intimately to the spirit than it had been destined to be.

On that basis we can now look deeply into the connection between the Mystery of Golgotha and the innermost powers of human nature and how it developed through the millennia. To really understand the Mystery of Golgotha historically in the right way, we must compare the relationship between body and soul that Ahriman and Lucifer decreed for us to the above-described relationship between soul and spirit. Interestingly, the Catholic Church, which was strongly influenced by the remnants of the impulses from the Academy of Gondishapur, decreed dogmatically in 869 at the eighth ecumenical council in Constantinople that it is not necessary to believe in the spirit.[†] The rulers of the church issued this decree because they did not want to have to enlighten everyone about the Mystery of Golgotha, but wanted to cover it in darkness instead. Thus, in 869 the Catholic Church practically abolished the spirit. The new dogma that was instituted at that time stipulates that believing in the spirit is not necessary; believing in body and soul is fully sufficient. In addition, it was stipulated that the soul has something spirit-like in it also. Essentially, then, the Catholic Church back then did away with the insight that we are made up of body, soul, and spirit, and it did so essentially under the influence of the Academy of Gondishapur. As you can see, history is not always in truth the way it is presented for everyday ordinary use and for this or that purpose. As we've seen, the Mystery of Golgotha brought human beings closer to the spirit. As a result, two forces coexist in all of us: the one that makes us deathlike in our soul and the one that frees us from death by leading us inwardly to the spirit.

As I've explained, the atheist tendency in us is a kind of disease, and we all carry the disposition for it inside us simply on account of having a physical body and living in a civilized society. Nevertheless, according to spiritual science, denying God, being an atheist, is a disease, and everyone is susceptible to developing it. Only when we find our way to God through Christ can we truly say that we're not denying God. Just as the body carries a tendency to sickness within it, a tendency to deny God, so we also have a wholesome, healing force within us, because as a result of the Mystery of Golgotha we have the Christ power within, as I've often described before. And Christ is our savior and healer in the true sense of the word, the one who heals the sicknesses that can make us into atheists. Christ is the remedy against the denial of God, the healer of the inner sickness I've described.

In many ways, our time is a recapitulation and renewal of what happened in the past, partly through the Mystery of Golgotha, partly through the events of 333, and partly through those of 666. There are very specific consequences involved here, and to properly understand the Mystery of Golgotha we must be clear that it cannot be understood at all with the powers we develop by living in a physical body between birth and death. Even Christ's contemporaries, his apostles and disciples, were not able to understand it on the basis of their human powers until the third century, that is, long after their death. All these things play a part in our development and give rise to many different turns of events, among them the following. We're in a very different position in our time than Christ's contemporaries or the people who lived in the subsequent centuries up to the seventh century. After all, we're living in the fifth post-Atlantean epoch, which is already far advanced; we're living in the twentieth century. This means that by the time we are born as soul and leave the spiritual world to enter the sensory world, we have had many experiences in the spiritual realm during the centuries before that birth. Just as Christ's contemporaries did not come to a full understanding of the Mystery of Golgotha until many centuries later, so we then experience the same thing many centuries before we are born, except in the reverse, as a mirror image. This applies only to people born in our time, all of whom carry with them at birth a sort of pale reflection of the Mystery of Golgotha, which is a mirror image of what people experienced in the spiritual world hundreds of years after Mystery of Golgotha. While we can only perceive this impulse if we have spiritual, supersensory perception, we can all experience the effects of it in ourselves. And by consciously and attentively experiencing this impulse, we can find the answer to the question we started with, namely, the question of how we can find our way to Christ.

To find Christ we need to have the following experiences: first, the experience of striving for self-knowledge. We must strive to know ourselves as well as we can within the constraints of our individual personality. And if we sincerely strive for self-knowledge, we will have to admit that we cannot really grasp what we're striving for. Our capacity to understand cannot keep up with what we're aiming for; we thus feel powerless in regard to our striving. This is a very important experience, and all of us, as we examine ourselves honestly in the process of gaining self-knowledge, should feel this sense of powerlessness. Feeling powerless in this connection is healthy, for this feeling is nothing other than the awareness of a disease. After all, being sick and not feeling or knowing it is usually a sign of a particularly serious illness. By feeling our powerlessness to come to God on our own at any time in our life, we feel the above-mentioned sickness within us, the sickness that was implanted in us. And our sense of the sickness also tells us that because of the way our body is in the present time, our soul would be doomed to die with the body if nothing stepped in to save it. When we have immersed ourselves for some time in this intense feeling of powerlessness, a change will occur. This change comes from experiencing the sudden realization that if we don't abandon ourselves to what we can achieve through the powers of our physical body alone, but instead give ourselves over to what the spirit offers us, then we can overcome this inner death of the soul. We will then be able to find our soul again and to connect with the spirit. Once we get beyond the feeling of powerlessness, we'll experience, on the one hand, the nothingness of existence and, on the other hand, the glorification of existence based only on ourselves. In our powerlessness, we become aware of the sickness. At the same time, as we experience the powerlessness and how our soul has become death-like, we also feel the Savior, the saving and healing power within us. As we sense the presence of the Savior within us, we realize that we carry something in our soul that can rise from the dead at any time through our own inner experience. These two experiences will lead us to finding Christ in our soul.

This is the experience that awaits us in the future, as Angelus Silesius had already realized when he wrote the following profoundly meaningful words:†

In vain the Cross on Golgotha
Was raised—thou hast not any part

144 * DEATH AS METAMORPHOSIS OF LIFE

In its deliverance unless
It be raised up within thy heart.[†]

The cross of Golgotha is raised within us when we feel the two
polar opposites: the powerlessness of our body and the resurrection
through our spirit. This inner experience consisting of two parts is
what truly leads us to an understanding of the Mystery of Golgotha.
Regarding this pivotal event, we cannot excuse our failure to understand it by pleading that we lack supersensory abilities. We don't need
those. All we really need is to practice self-reflection and be willing
to reflect on ourselves and to fight the arrogance that is so prevalent
these days. It's generally this arrogance that prevents us from noticing that the more we rely exclusively on our own powers, the more
arrogant we become in regard to them. When our arrogance renders
us blind and numb so that we don't notice that our own powers make
us powerless, then we will not able to experience the inner death and
resurrection. Then we will never feel the way Angelus Silesius did, as
he expressed in these words:

In vain the Cross on Golgotha
Was raised—thou hast not any part
In its deliverance unless
It be raised up within thy heart.

Once we can feel ourselves powerless and then being restored from
powerlessness, we will be so fortunate as to have a real relationship to
Christ Jesus, for the above-described experience is a recapitulation of
what we've experienced centuries earlier in the spiritual world. And
the mirror image of that earlier experience is what we must be looking
for in our soul here on the physical plane. If you look inside, you'll
find powerlessness. Seek, and you will find—and after the powerlessness, you will find the release from powerlessness, the resurrection of
the soul to the spirit.

It is important to not let yourself be misled by what certain mystical movements and even religious denominations are preaching these
days. For example, what Harnack is saying about Christ is not true

simply because what he says can be applied just as well to God as such—read it for yourself and you'll see that everything he states could just as well and with as much justification be said about the God of the Jews and about the God of the Muslims and so on.[†] Many of those who call themselves "awakened" these days claim, "I experience God within me," but they only experience God the Father, and even that is only a muted, pallid experience because they do not realize that they are inwardly sick and are merely parroting traditional platitudes. Johannes Müller is a clear example of this trend.[†] In any case, those "awakened" people do not have Christ, for experiencing Christ is not a matter feeling God in our soul; rather, we must feel both death in our soul on account of the body *and* the resurrection of the soul through the spirit. Anyone can claim to feel God within himself or herself—even the purely rhetorical theosophists make that claim. However, only when we go beyond that to the two experiences of powerlessness and resurrection from that powerlessness, do we come to a true Christ experience. Then we're also on the spiritual path to understanding the Mystery of Golgotha; we can then find the forces that stimulate certain spiritual powers and lead us to the Mystery of Golgotha. You see, there's no need to worry about finding Christ through our own direct experience, for we have found him when we've found ourselves again after the experience of powerlessness—that is, when we fully experience and overcome that powerlessness. That feeling of powerlessness or nothingness will naturally pass when we honestly and without arrogance think about our own powers and abilities. And this feeling is indispensable and must precede the Christ impulse. Some clever mystics believe that finding the higher "I," the God-"I," within their "I" makes them true Christians. However, this is a far cry from what Christianity really is. Christianity must be based on this sentence by Silesius:

In vain the Cross on Golgotha
Was raised—thou hast not any part
In its deliverance unless
It be raised up within thy heart.

The details of life confirm that what I'm saying here is true, and we can then move from these details to the all-suffusing feeling of powerlessness and the resurrection from that powerlessness. My dear friends, we would do well to take the first step toward that feeling of our physical body's powerlessness when confronted with divine truth, and we can do so fairly easily by cultivating the following realization. Doubtlessly, in the depths of our soul we're all inclined toward the truth, and consequently toward expressing that truth. Now, precisely at the moment when we're about to speak the truth and reflect on our intention to speak the truth, that is when we can take that first step toward the experience of powerlessness described above. As we reflect on what we mean by speaking the truth, we come to the strange realization that Schiller already put in words in one of his "Votive Tablets": "Soon as the soul 'gins to *speak*, then can the *soul* speak no more!"† In other words, in the process of being put into words, into language, what we inwardly really experience as truth gets blunted. It is not killed or deadened in the process, but it begins to dull. Moreover, if we've learned anything about language, we know that proper names, words that designate one and only one thing, are the only correct words for the thing each designates. As soon as we use general terms, whether they're nouns, verbs, or adjectives, we're no longer articulating the whole truth. Indeed, truth then means realizing that with each sentence we say, we're essentially and necessarily deviating from the truth.

In spiritual science we try to rise again from this realization that with every one of our statements we're expressing an untruth by adopting the method I've often described for you. As I've said before, in spiritual science what matters is not so much *what* is said but rather *how* it is said. After all, what we say would also be subject to the feeling of powerlessness. You can see for yourself what I mean when you trace in my lectures and even in my writings how every topic is described from more than one viewpoint, how everything is presented from various angles, because only then can we come close to understanding these topics. If you think that the words themselves are more than a kind of eurythmy, you're very much mistaken. Words are really nothing more than eurythmy carried out by the larynx with the help of the air. They are essentially merely gestures, except that they're not made with hands and feet but with the larynx instead. Thus, we must realize that in speaking we are merely gesturing toward something, and to develop the right relationship to truth we must understand every word as a gesture toward what we want to express. That is, our words are gestures, pointers, or signs, and that is also what eurythmy teaches us. Eurythmy essentially turns the whole person into a larynx so that we express with our whole body what normally only the larynx expresses.[†] Thus, in eurhythmy we experience firsthand that even when we speak with sounds, we're really only making gestures.

For example, when we say the words "father" or "mother" in general, we can only express ourselves truthfully if the other person, our dialog partner, lives as deeply in the same social element as we do and thus understands our gesture. We rise again from the powerlessness we can feel regarding language—we're resurrected from that powerlessness and overcome it—only when we understand that in the moment we open our mouth to speak, we must already be Christian. What has become of words, of the Logos, in the course of history can be understood only if we reconnect the Logos with Christ. That is, we must realize that as our body becomes the vehicle of speech, it forces the truth downward, and as result part of it dies on our lips. We can make it come to life again in Christ when we understand that we must spiritualize it—that is, mentally, in our thinking, we must include the spirit rather than taking in only the words as such. This is what we must learn, my dear friends.

I hope to be able to say more about this in tomorrow's public talk, but I'm not sure if there will be enough time.[†] In any case, I'd like to speak about this to you today and hope it won't bother you if you hear it again tomorrow. First of all, I'd like to say to you what I've said in many public lectures where I've described what you can find if you thoroughly study the essays written by Woodrow Wilson, as I have studied them.[†] Wilson wrote very interesting essays about American history, literature, and life. In a sense, he provided an impressive presentation of the American development from East to West, and he did so as an American, from his American perspective. In fact, his essays, which he originally presented as lectures and then wrote down, make compelling reading. They're entitled *Mere Literature*, and we can really learn what Americans are like by reading this book because Wilson is the prototypical American. In an objective comparison, I've put passages from Wilson's essays next to comparable ones from the writings of Herman Grimm, who can be described as a prototypical German, or even Central European, of the nineteenth century—in fact, I find Grimm's writing style as appealing as I find Wilson's distasteful, but that's just my personal opinion.[†] I love the way Grimm writes, but Wilson's style just grates on my ears; still, we can be completely objective about this: Wilson, the prototypical American, writes brilliantly, magnificently, about the development and history of the American people.

However, something else must be considered when comparing Wilson's essays with those by Grimm, especially in their treatment of the method of history. There we find that some of Wilson's statements are almost identical, word for word, with Grimm's. Likewise, several of Grimm's sentences would fit easily into Wilson's essay and not change the meaning. Nevertheless, any direct borrowing is out of the question. I assure you that I'm not talking about borrowing or plagiarizing here. Instead, here we can learn firsthand, without becoming philistines or bourgeois, that when two people say the same thing, it's not the same at all. The problem here is that Wilson describes his fellow countrymen in a much more forceful, lively, and suggestive way than Hermann Grimm ever did in his historical method; and yet, Woodrow Wilson is practically speaking in Grimm's words. We have to wonder what's going on here, what causes this. As we study the matter more closely, what we find is that Hermann Grimm's style shows that every one of Grimm's sentence is the result of a hard personal, individual struggle. Grimm, a luminary of nineteenth-century culture, wrote about all kinds of things, but everything ultimately grew directly out of his consciousness soul. Wilson's descriptions are brilliant, but as though possessed by something in his own subconscious. Indeed, there are traces of demonic possession here; there is something in his subconscious that inspired him, that fed him what he then wrote down. This demon expresses itself in a special way in an American of the twentieth century, speaks through Wilson's soul. That is the great and mighty reality we must become aware of.

However, nowadays people are so lazy that when they read something, their response is usually to say that they've read the same thing elsewhere too—in other words, they focus only on the content. But now is the time when we must all learn that the content by itself doesn't matter as much anymore; instead, what matters is that we understand others based on their words, and we must see those words as nothing more than gestures. Thus, we must know who makes the gestures, for they determine what the words mean. Truly, this is something we must get used to because it is one of the greatest mysteries of even ordinary life, my friends. There's a great difference between sentences that have been struggled for and wrestled with by the personal "I," and those that have been given in some way as inspiration from above or below. Of course, we'll find sentences resulting from inspiration to be more suggestive and compelling, because those that have been struggled for require that we also struggle in reading them. The time is coming when we will have to move away from merely looking at the literal, verbatim meaning of what appears before our soul, and instead must consider the person who is saying this or that. That is, we must focus not on the outer physical personality, but rather on the whole human-spiritual context.

Accordingly, this must be our answer to the question of how to find Christ. For Christ cannot be found by means of any strange woolgathering or through convenient mysticism. We can find Christ only if we have the courage to take our place in the midst of life; and that means that we must also feel the above-mentioned powerlessness in regard to language, powerlessness that our body has brought upon us because it has become the bearer of speech. That experience of powerlessness must be followed by the resurrection of the spirit in the word. That's the answer. It's not just a matter of "the letter kills, but the Spirit gives life," another sentence that has often been misunderstood.† Instead, it's already the sound that kills, and for the Spirit to give life again, we must connect our concrete, individual experience to Christ and the Mystery of Golgotha. Thus, the first step to finding Christ is this: seek, but not just by looking for the meaning of pretty words here and there—that's all people are used to these days; instead, we must seek the human context, looking at how the words emerge out of the place they are spoken from. This will become increasingly important in the future. If more of us would consider this, people wouldn't urge us so often to read this or that because the author appears to write completely in line with Anthroposophy or Theosophy. It doesn't matter so much what words are on the page; what matters is the spirit out of which a person speaks. Anthroposophy is not about spreading words but about bringing a new spirit, and this is the spirit that, beginning with the twentieth century, must be the spirit of Christianity.

My dear friends, this is what I wanted to add to what we'd talked about a week ago. I am very glad it was possible to do this, and that I could talk to you again about these issues that concern us all. I hope that we will soon be able to continue these talks here in Zurich. On this note, let us always remember even when we are apart that as Anthroposophists we are always together in our soul. Let us remain united faithfully in this way, in the spirit of humanity that shall prevail.

REFERENCE NOTES

Page 1, "I would like to continue with our reflections from a previous talk"
Lecture titled "The Relationship between the Living and the Dead," November 9, 1916 (CW 168).

Page 2, "my Vienna lectures"
Lecture titled "Inner Being of Man and Life between Death and Rebirth," in *Inner Nature of Man and the Life between Death and a New Birth*, trsl. Charles Davy and D. Osmond (London: Anthroposophical Publishing, 1959) (CW 153).

Page 3, *"Theosophy"*
Steiner, *Theosophy: An Introduction to the Spiritual Processes in Human Life and in the Cosmos* (1904), translated by Catherine E. Creeger (Great Barrington, MA: Steiner-Books, 1994) (CW 9). Cf. "The Three Worlds," 1. The World of the Soul.

Page 5, "tomorrow's public lecture"
Lecture titled, "Insights from Spiritual Science on the Ideas of Freedom and an Ethical Society," Bern, November 30, 1917. Unpublished, inclusion in CW 72 planned.

Page 10, "even in yesterday's public lecture"
Lecture titled "The Workings of the Soul Forces in Us and their Connection to Our Eternal Being: Insights from Spiritual Science on the Essence of the Human Being," Bern, November 28, 1917. Unpublished, inclusion in Collected Works 72 planned.

Page 13, "the historical proofs of Christ's existence fill a quarto page at most"
Adolf von Harnack (1851-1930) wrote: "Aside from a few important passage in the Apostle Paul's letters, our sources for the what Jesus preached are essentially the first three gospels. Everything else we know about the history and preaching of Jesus independently of these gospels will easily fit on a quarto page—that's how little we know." In *Das Wesen des Christentumes* (The Essence of Christianity), Leipzig, 1901.

Page 14, "a theologian wrote a remarkable book"
Albert Schweitzer, *The Quest of the Historical Jesus; A Critical Study of Its Progress From Reimarus to Wrede* (1906) (Minneapolis: Augsburg Fortress Publishers, 2001).

Page 15, "first Mystery Drama"
Steiner, "The Portal of Initiation" (1910) in *Four Mystery Dramas*, translated by Ruth and Hans Pusch (Great Barrington, MA: SteinerBooks, 2007) (CW 14).

Page 18, "the issue of the Socratic daimon"
In Plato, The Apology (of Socrates) in Plato's *Dialogues*.

Page 18, *"The Spiritual Guidance of the Individual and Humanity"*
Steiner, *The Spiritual Guidance of the Individual and Humanity: Some Results of Spiritual-Scientific Research into Human History and Development* (1911, based on 3 lectures, Copenhagen, June 1911), translated by Samuel Desch (Great Barrington, MA: SteinerBooks, 1991) (CW 15).

Page 18, *"Riddles of the Soul"*
See: Steiner, *Riddles of the Soul* (1917), trsl. W. Lindeman (Spring Valley, NY: Mercury Press, 1996) (CW 21). The second chapter of Steiner's book is titled "Max Dessoir on Anthroposophy" and is Steiner's response to Dessoir's criticism of Anthroposophy in his 1917 book *Vom Jenseits der Seele: Die Geheimwissenschaften in kritischer Betrachtung* (From the Far Side of the Soul: A Critical Consideration of the Occult Sciences).

Page 18, "the learned and scholarly fellow Max Dessoir"
Max Dessoir (1867-1947), German neo-Kantian philosopher and theorist of aesthetics with an interest in parapsychology.

Page 21, "even the pope ... has offered a program for peace"
On August 1, 1917, the third anniversary of the beginning of World War I, Pope Benedict XV called upon the warring nations to make peace.

Page 21, it is also crucial that we correctly read the signs of the times"
Cf. lectures held May 11-13, 1917, published in *Die geistigen Hintergründe des Ersten Weltkrieges* (The Spiritual Reasons Behind the First World War) (CW 174b).

Page 28, "How to Know Higher Worlds"
Steiner, *How to Know Higher Worlds: A Modern Path of Initiation*. Written in 1904-1905. Translated by Christopher Bamford (Great Barrington, MA: SteinerBooks, 1994) (CW 10). Previously titled *How to Achieve Knowledge of the Higher Worlds*.

Page 29, "the Old Testament practically forbids any contact with the dead"
See Deuteronomy 18:10-13: "There shall not be found among you any one who burns his son or his daughter as an offering, any one who practices divination, a soothsayer, or an augur, or a sorcerer, or a charmer, or a medium, a wizard, or a necromancer. For whoever does these things is an abomination to the Lord; and because of these abominable practices the Lord your God is driving them out before you." Cf. also 1 Samuel 28, on Samuel and the witch of Endor.

Page 31, "I talked about the outer human physical organism"
Steiner, *A Psychology of Body, Soul, and Spirit: Anthroposophy, Psychosophy,*

Pneumatosophy (12 lectures, Oct. 1909; Nov. 1910; Dec. 1911). Translated by Marjorie Spock (Great Barrington, MA: SteinerBooks, 1999) (CW 115).

Page 33, "Time here becomes space"
Richard Wagner (1813-1883); Steiner quotes the words of Gurnemanz in Act I of *Parsifal.*

Page 41, "And the words of the gospel apply particularly to those who have died"
Luke 17:20.

Page 48, "as I said in a public lecture in Stuttgart"
Lecture titled "Spiritual Man and the Questions of Freedom of Will and Immortality According to Findings of Spiritual Science," April 24, 1918. Cf. related lectures presented in Berlin on April 18 and 20, 1918, published in *Das Ewige in der Menschenseele: Unsterblichkeit und Freiheit* (The Eternal in the Human Soul: Immortality and Freedom) (CW 67).

Page 51, what Pythagoras meant by the muse of the spheres"
Pythagoras (582-493 B.C.E.). According to Steiner, the music of the spheres Pythagoras refers to is the "resounding of the spiritual world," lecture of August 31, 1906, published in *Founding a Science of the Spirit* (14 lectures, Stuttgart, August 22- September 4, 1906) (Great Barrington, MA: SteinerBooks, 1999) (CW 95).

Page 57, "As I've said in a previous lecture"
Lecture titled "The Mission of Devotion," October 20, 1909, published in *Transforming the Soul,* vol. 1 (9 lectures, Berlin, October 14- December 9, 1909). Translated by Pauline Wehrle (Great Barrington, MA: SteinerBooks, 2006) (CW 58).

Page 58, "Woodrow Wilson"
Woodrow Wilson (1856-1924), president of the United States from 1913-1921.

Page 60, "we're gathered here to celebrate"
Steiner gave this lecture on the occasion of the official opening of the Anthroposophical Society's branch in the city of Ulm.

Page 62, "the economic and industrial life...also needs a soul"
Cf. the lecture of October 30, 1913 in Berlin, published in *Die Geisteswissenschaft als Lebensgut* (Spiritual Science as a Blessing for Life) (CW 63). In particular, see the following sentence: "The goal of spiritual science is to permeate the body of our culture with soul and spirit."

Page 63, "Society for Ethical Culture"
The German Society for Ethical Culture was founded in 1892 by W. Förster

and Georg von Gizycki. See Steiner, *Autobiography: Chapters in the Course of My Life: 1861-1907* (1924) (Great Barrington, MA: SteinerBooks, 2006) (CW 28); and also Steiner, *Gesammelte Aufsätze zur Kultur- und Zeitgeschichte, 1887-1901* (Collected Essays on Cultural and Political History) (CW 31), for Steiner's relationship to that society.

Page 65, "Friedrich Nietzsche exemplifies this very well"
Friedrich Nietzsche (1844-1900); see Steiner, *Friedrich Nietzsche: Fighter for Freedom* (1895) (Blauvelt, New York: Garber Communications, 1985) (CW 5).

Page 66, "the earth as a whole has its task to fulfill"
Cf. Steiner, *An Outline of Esoteric Science* (1910), translated by Catherine Creeger (Great Barrington, MA: SteinerBooks, 1997) (CW 13).

Page 68, "simple man from Nazareth"
Gustav Frenssen (1863-1945), Protestant pastor and novelist, spoke of "the simple hero of Nazareth" in his sermons, published in *Dorfpredigten* (Village Sermons) in 1900.

Page 69, "against erosion by the West"
In the ninth century the Eastern Church (Byzantium) began to separate from Rome.

Page 69, "Leninism and Trotskyism"
In October 1917 Lenin (1870-1924) and Trotsky (1879-1940) led the Bolshevik revolution in Russia.

Page 70, Rabindranath Tagore"
Rabindranath Tagore (1861-1941), Indian poet and philosopher. His lecture "The Spirit of Japan" appeared in a translation by Helene Meyer-Franck in "Preussische Jahrbücher," vol. 171, no. 1, in January 1918.

Page 72, "limits of knowledge"
Since Kant modern philosophy has emphasized the limits of knowledge (cf. the scientific slogan propounded by Emil BuBois-Reymond: *"Ignoramus et ignorabimus"*—We do not know and we shall never know). Cf. Steiner, *Intuitive Thinking as a Spiritual Path: A Philosophy of Freedom* (1894), trsl. Michael Lipson (Great Barrington, MA: SteinerBooks, 1995) (CW 4); *Riddles of Philosophy* (1914) (Spring Valley, NY: Anthroposophic Press, 1973) (CW 18); *The Boundaries of Natural Science*, trsl. Frederick Amrine and Konrad Oberhuber (Spring Valley, NY: Anthroposophic Press, 1983) (CW 322).

Page 73, *"The Mystery of the Human Being"*
Steiner, *Vom Menschenrätsel* (On the Human Being as Enigma) (1916) (CW 20).

Page 73, "Herder's description"
Johann Gottfried Herder, *Älteste Urkunde des Menschengeschlechts* (Oldest Records of the Human Race) (1774-76), part 1, plan 3, p. 70: "The oldest and most glorious revelation of God appears before you every morning as a fact" in "Picture of Dawn, Picture of the beginning Day." Cf. also Herder's poem "Die Schöpfung: Ein Morgengesang" (The Creation: A Morning Song), 1773.

Page 73, "Ku Hung-Ming"
M. A. Ku Hung-Ming (1857-1928), Chinese scholar and official. His book *The Spirit of the Chinese People* (1915) became available in German translation in 1916.

Page 74, "a man was hired"
The retired Prussian secretary of state and minister of finance, Georg Kreuzwendedich Baron of Rheinbaben was chosen as head of the Goethe Society.

Page 74, "a rather strange essay by a very learned man"
Franz Boll collaborated with Carl Bezold on vol. 638 in the series. The book was titled *Sternglaube und Sterndeutung: Die Geschichte und das Wesen der Astrologie* (Belief in the Stars and their Interpretation: History and Nature of Astrology) and published in 1918.

Page 75, "Fritz Mauthner ranted and raved about that book"
Fritz Mauthner in the newspaper *Berliner Tageblatt*, 47, no. 161, 1918. Evening edition of March 28.

Page 75, "the author of the book published a correction"
Boll's response in the same paper, no. 192, morning edition of April 16, 1918.

Page 86, "Lloyd George"
David Lloyd George (1863-1945), minister since 1905, head of government from 1916 to 1922.

Page 86, "Campbell-Bannerman administration"
Sir Henry Campbell-Bannerman (1836-1908), prime minister of England from 1906 to 1908.

Page 87, "Matthais Erzberger"
Matthias Erzberger (1865-1921), statesman.

Page 87, "he described his early years up to the move to Weimar"
Johann Wolfgang von Goethe, *Autobiography: Truth and Fiction Relating to My Life*, trsl. John Oxenford. Available at Project Gutenberg: www.gutenberg.org/etext/5733

Page 88, "I've established Goethe's personal relationship to his Faust"
Steiner, *Goethe's Standard of the Soul, as illustrated in Faust and The Green Snake and the Beautiful Lily*, trsl. D. Osmond (London: Rudolf Steiner Publishing, 1925) (CW 22).

Page 88, "As wise as when I entered school…"
Johann Wolfgang von Goethe, *Faust*, Act I, in *Faust: A Tragedy*, trsl. with notes by Charles T. Brooks, 7th ed. (Boston: Ticknor & Fields, 1856). Available at Project Gutenberg: http://www.gutenberg.org/files/14460/14460-8.txt. All further quotes from Faust are taken from this source.

Page 89, "Like the wind I sweep!"
Faust, Act I, night.

Page 89, "Not me!"
Faust, Act I, night.

Page 90, "Becloudig Heaven's warm glow."
Faust, Act I, Martha's garden.

Page 91, "Jakob Minor wrote an interesting book"
Jakob Minor (1855-1912), scholar of German literature. His two-volume work on Goethe's *Faust* was published in 1901.

Page 92, "There is a lot of talk these days about the subconscious"
C. G. Jung, "On the Psychology of the Unconscious," in: *Two Essays on Analytical Psychology* (1966 revised 2d ed. Collected Works vol. 7) (London: Routledge, 1966). German: Zurich 1917.

Page 94, "Otto Weininger"
Otto Weininger (1880-1903), philosopher. In 1903 he wrote *Sex and Character: An Investigation of Fundamental Principles*, trsl. Ladislaus Löb (Bloomington: Indiana University Press, 2005).

Page 95, "In his last book"
Weininger, *A Translation of Weininger's Über die letzten Dinge (1904/1907)/ On Last Things*, trsl. Steven Burns (Lewiston, NY: Edwin Mellen Press, 2001): "Perhaps no memory of our state *prior* to birth is possible because we have sunk so low through being born: we have lost consciousness, and demand entirely instinctively to be born, without rational decision and without knowledge, and that is why we know nothing at all of this past."

Page 97, "Riddles of the Soul"
Steiner, *Riddles of the Soul* (1917), trsl. W. Lindeman (Spring Valley, NY: Mercury Press, 1996 (CW 21). See relevant note on page 18.

Page 97, "in the most recent issue"
Kantstudien, philosophical journal devoted to Kant studies See vol. 22, no. 4, p. 464, review of Dessoir's book *Vom Jenseits der Seele* by Emil Utitz, Rostock.

Page 97, "that essay"
Max Dessoir, *Vom Jenseits der Seele: Die Geheimwissenschaften in kritischer Betrachtung* (From the Far Side of the Soul: A Critical Consideration of the Occult Sciences), 1917. See relevant note on page 18.

Page 98, "the Roman empire…was getting poorer and poorer"
On the decline of Roman coinage in the early Middle Ages, the debasement of currency, etc., see John Kenneth Galbraith, *Money: Whence it came, where it went*, rev. ed. (New York: Houghton Mifflin, 2004).

Page 99, "my talks in Berlin some time ago…primarily the numbers twelve and seven"
Steiner, *Human and Cosmic Thought* (4 lectures, Berlin, January 20-23, 1914) (Great Barrington, MA: SteinerBooks, 1991) (CW 151).

Page 100, "an attempt to list and classify all worldviews now in existence"
Ernst Rolffs, "The World War as Worldview Critique," *Preussische Jahrbücher* (Prussian Yearbooks), vol. 172, no. 3, Berlin, June 1918.

Page 102, "this is the book by Oscar Hertwig"
Oscar Hertwig (1849-1922), anatomist. In 1916 he published *Das Werden der Organismen: Eine Widerlegung der Darwinschen Zufallslehre* (The Origin of Organisms: A Refutation of Darwin's Theory of Chance), and in 1918 *Zur Abwehr des ethischen, sozialen und des politischen Darwinismus* (Against Darwinism in Ethics, Society, and Politics) followed.

Page 102, "Gibbon…wrote his masterful history"
Edward Gibbon (1737-1794), English historian. *History of the Decline and Fall of the Roman Empire*, 6 vols. (London 1782-88).

Page 103, "Treitschke claimed…the real driving forces of history"
Heinrich von Treitschke (1834-1896), German historian. "The lies currently spread abroad in English and French newspapers—both deliberately and inadvertently—serve as depressing evidence for Treitschke's often repeated claim that passion and stupidity are the great driving powers of history" (E. Rolffs, "The World War as Worldview Critique," *Preussische Jahrbücher* (Prussian Yearbooks), vol. 172, no. 3, Berlin, June 1918.)

Page 105, "Hermann von Helmholtz"
Hermann von Helmholtz (1821-1894), physiologist and physicist. Inventor of the ophthalmoscope.

Page 110, *"An Outline of Esoteric Science"*
Steiner, *An Outline of Esoteric Science* (1910), translated by Catherine Creeger (Great Barrington, MA: SteinerBooks, 1997) (CW 13). See also reference on page 66.

Page 125, "we should not sleep through what will be carried into our conscious life…"
The notes on which the text is based were incomplete in this passage. The meaning here is supported by a similar passage in chapter 2 of *The Spiritual Guidance of the Individual and Humanity: Some Results of Spiritual-Scientific Research into Human History and Development.* See relevant note on page 18.

Page 130, from my book *Christianity as Mystical Fact"*
Steiner, *Christianity as Mystical Fact and the Mysteries of Antiquity* (1902), trsl. Andrew Welburn (Great Barrington, MA: SteinerBooks, 2006) (CW 8).

Page 130, "Adolf Harnack, who is a renowned theologian"
Adolf von Harnack (1851-1930). See note for page 13.

Page 131, "how to use the intellectual or mind soul in freedom"
See Gotthold Ephraim Lessing, *The Education of the Human Race* (1780).

Page 133, "Tertullian"
Tertullian (ca. 160- ca. 220), church writer. His work in defense of the Christians is titled "Apologetic and Practical Treatises" and is available at http://www.ccel.org/ccel/schaff/anf03.v.vii.v.html.

Page 133, "I believe what is foolish and not what is reasonable"
Steiner quotes from memory. Translation available at http://www.ccel.org/ccel/schaff/anf03.v.vii.v.html

Page 135, it is by all means to be believed, because it is absurd!"
See http://www.ccel.org/ccel/schaff/anf03.v.vii.v.html

Page 135, "we must believe it precisely because it is impossible"
See http://www.ccel.org/ccel/schaff/anf03.v.vii.v.html

Page 136, "read those passages about the year 666"
Cf. Book of Revelation 13:18.

Page 137, "the emperor Justinian"
Justinian (482-565), Eastern Roman emperor.

Page 137, "Zeno Isauricus had already expelled"
Zeno Isauricus, emperor from 474 to 491. In 489 he issued a decree closing the School of Edessa.

Page 137, "at the Academy of Gondishapur"
Regarding the Academy of Gondishapur, cf. Steiner's lectures of October 12 and 16, 1918 in *Die Polarität von Dauer und Entwicklung* (The Polarity of Duration and Development) (CW 184), and H. H. Schöffler, *Die Akademie von Gondischapur: Aristoteles auf dem Wege in den Orient* (The Academy of Gondishapur: Aristotle's Path to the Orient) (Stuttgart, 1980).

Page 138, "Muhammad"
Muhammad (ca. 570-632).

Page 139, "Paul had much to say"
Cf. 2 Corinthians 12:7.

Page 141, "at the eighth council in Constantinople"
This council was primarily convened against the Patriarch Photius. In its "Canones contra Photium," the council decreed in Can. 11 that human beings do not have "two souls" but *"unam animam rationabilem et intellectualem,"* that is, human beings have only one rational understanding soul. The Catholic philosopher Otto Willmann, whom Steiner held in high esteem, wrote, "It was on account of the Gnostics' misuse of the Pauline distinction between the spiritual and psychical human being, presenting the former as an expression of their perfection and the latter as the representative of Christians caught up in Church laws, that the Church explicitly rejected the trichotomy" in section 54 of "Christian Idealism as a Completion of Antiquity," vol. 2 of *Geschichte des Idealismus* (History of Idealism), 3 vols. (Braunschweig, 1894).

Steiner often spoke of the Council of Constantinople and its significant decision, for example in returned to the importance of this Council's decision, for example, in *The Influences of Lucifer and Ahriman: Human Responsibility for the Earth*, trsl. D. Osmond (Great Barrington, MA: SteinerBooks, 1993), Collected Works 191; *The Archangel Michael* (Great Barrington, MA: SteinerBooks Press, 1995), Collected Works 194; and Collected Works 203.

Page 143, Angeles Silesius...wrote the following ...words"
Angelus Silesius (Johann Scheffler, 1624-1677), German mystic and poet. From Silesius, *The Cherubinic Wanderer*, trans. with intro. by J. E. Crawford Flitch (1932), available at http://www.sacred-texts.com/chr/sil/scw/scw05.htm.

Page 145, "Johannes Müller"
Johannes Müller (1864-1949), philosopher of life, founded the Freistatt persönlichen Lebens für Suchende jeder Richtung und Herkunft (Sanctuary of personal life for seekers from any direction and origin) at castle Elmau in Upper Bavaria. Wrote numerous treatises on religious and social issues.

Page 146, "Soon as the soul 'gins to *speak*..."
See Schiller's poems from the third period, "Votive Tablets" in *Tapio Riikonen*

and David Widger, *Schiller's Poems*; available at Project Gutenberg: http://www.gutenberg.org/dirs/6/7/9/6796/6796.txt

Page 147, "Eurythmy essentially turns the whole person into a larynx"
See Steiner, *Eurythmie: Die Offenbarung der sprechenden Seele* (Eurythmy: Revelation of the Speaking Soul), introductory talks to various eurythmy performances. In part, this collection is translated in *Eurythmy: Its Birth and Development*, trsl. A. Stott (Weobley, UK: Anastasi, 2002) (CW 277).

Page 147, "I hope to say more about this in tomorrow's public talk"
See Steiner's lecture of October 17, 1918, "Modern History in the Light of Spiritual Science," in *Anthroposophy Has Something to Add to Modern Sciences*, trsl. Anna Meuss (Lower Beechmont, Australia: Completion Press, 2004) (CW 73). Steiner takes up the topic again in that lecture.

Page 147, "essays written by Woodrow Wilson"
Woodrow Wilson, *Mere Literature and Other Essays*, repr. (University Press of the Pacific, 2004).

Page 148, "I find Grimm's style of writing as appealing as I find Wilson's distasteful"
Herman Grimm (1838-1901), art historian. On the comparison of Herman Grimm and W. Wilson, see also Steiner's lecture of March 30, 1918 in Berlin in *Erdensterben und Weltenleben: Anthroposophische Lebensgaben, Bewusstseins-Notwendigkeiten für Gegenwart und Zukunft*, in part translated in *Earthly Death and Cosmic Life*, trsl. Charles Davy and D. Osmond (London: Rudolf Steiner Press 1964) (CW 181).

Page 149, "the letter kills, but the Spirit gives life"
2 Corinthians 3:6.

RUDOLF STEINER'S COLLECTED WORKS

The German Edition of Rudolf Steiner's Collected Works (the Gesamtausgabe [GA] published by Rudolf Steiner Verlag, Dornach, Switzerland) presently runs to over 354 titles, organized either by type of work (written or spoken), chronology, audience (public or other), or subject (education, art, etc.). For ease of comparison, the Collected Works in English [CW] follows the German organization exactly. A complete listing of the CWs follows with literal translations of the German titles. Other than in the case of the books published in his lifetime, titles were rarely given by Rudolf Steiner himself, and were often provided by the editors of the German editions. The titles in English are not necessarily the same as the German; and, indeed, over the past seventy-five years have frequently been different, with the same book sometimes appearing under different titles.

For ease of identification and to avoid confusion, we suggest that readers looking for a title should do so by CW number. Because the work of creating the Collected Works of Rudolf Steiner is an ongoing process, with new titles being published every year, we have not indicated in this listing which books are presently available. To find out what titles in the Collected Works are currently in print, please check our website at www.steinerbooks.org, or write to SteinerBooks 610 Main Street, Great Barrington, MA 01230:

Written Work

CW 1	Goethe: Natural-Scientific Writings, Introduction, with Footnotes and Explanations in the text by Rudolf Steiner
CW 2	Outlines of an Epistemology of the Goethean World View, with Special Consideration of Schiller
CW 3	Truth and Science
CW 4	The Philosophy of Freedom
CW 4a	Documents to "The Philosophy of Freedom"
CW 5	Friedrich Nietzsche, A Fighter against His Own Time
CW 6	Goethe's Worldview
CW 6a	Now in CW 30
CW 7	Mysticism at the Dawn of Modern Spiritual Life and Its Relationship with Modern Worldviews
CW 8	Christianity as Mystical Fact and the Mysteries of Antiquity
CW 9	Theosophy: An Introduction into Supersensible World Knowledge and Human Purpose
CW 10	How Does One Attain Knowledge of Higher Worlds?
CW 11	From the Akasha-Chronicle
CW 12	Levels of Higher Knowledge

CW 13	Occult Science in Outline
CW 14	Four Mystery Dramas
CW 15	The Spiritual Guidance of the Individual and Humanity
CW 16	A Way to Human Self-Knowledge: Eight Meditations
CW 17	The Threshold of the Spiritual World. Aphoristic Comments
CW 18	The Riddles of Philosophy in Their History, Presented as an Outline
CW 19	Contained in CW 24
CW 20	The Riddles of the Human Being: Articulated and Unarticulated in the Thinking, Views and Opinions of a Series of German and Austrian Personalities
CW 21	The Riddles of the Soul
CW 22	Goethe's Spiritual Nature And Its Revelation In "Faust" and through the "Fairy Tale of the Snake and the Lily"
CW 23	The Central Points of the Social Question in the Necessities of Life in the Present and the Future
CW 24	Essays Concerning the Threefold Division of the Social Organism and the Period 1915-1921
CW 25	Cosmology, Religion and Philosophy
CW 26	Anthroposophical Leading Thoughts
CW 27	Fundamentals for Expansion of the Art of Healing according to Spiritual-Scientific Insights
CW 28	The Course of My Life
CW 29	Collected Essays on Dramaturgy, 1889-1900
CW 30	Methodical Foundations of Anthroposophy: Collected Essays on Philosophy, Natural Science, Aesthetics and Psychology, 1884-1901
CW 31	Collected Essays on Culture and Current Events, 1887-1901
CW 32	Collected Essays on Literature, 1884-1902
CW 33	Biographies and Biographical Sketches, 1894-1905
CW 34	Lucifer-Gnosis: Foundational Essays on Anthroposophy and Reports from the Periodicals "Lucifer" and "Lucifer-Gnosis," 1903-1908
CW 35	Philosophy and Anthroposophy: Collected Essays, 1904-1923
CW 36	The Goetheanum-Idea in the Middle of the Cultural Crisis of the Present: Collected Essays from the Periodical "Das Goetheanum," 1921-1925
CW 37	Now in CWs 260a and 251
CW 38	Letters, Vol. 1: 1881-1890
CW 39	Letters, Vol. 2: 1890-1925
CW 40	Truth-Wrought Words
CW 40a	Sayings, Poems and Mantras; Supplementary Volume
CW 42	Now in CWs 264-266

CW 78   Anthroposophy, Its Roots of Knowledge and Fruits for Life
CW 79   The Reality of the Higher Worlds
CW 80   Public lectures in various cities, 1922
CW 81   Renewal-Impulses for Culture and Science–Berlin College Course
CW 82   So that the Human Being Can Become a Complete Human Being
CW 83   Western and Eastern World-Contrast. Paths to Understanding It
          through Anthroposophy
CW 84   What Did the Goetheanum Intend and What Should
          Anthroposophy Do?

Lectures to the Members of the Anthroposophical Society

CW 88   Concerning the Astral World and Devachan
CW 89   Consciousness–Life–Form. Fundamental Principles of a Spiritual-
          Scientific Cosmology
CW 90   Participant Notes from the Lectures during the Years 1903-1905
CW 91   Participant Notes from the Lectures during the Years 1903-1905
CW 92   The Occult Truths of Ancient Myths and Sagas
CW 93   The Temple Legend and the Golden Legend
CW 93a   Fundamentals of Esotericism
CW 94   Cosmogony. Popular Occultism. The Gospel of John.
          The Theosophy in the Gospel of John
CW 95   At the Gates of Theosophy
CW 96   Origin-Impulses of Spiritual Science. Christian Esotericism in the
          Light of New Spirit-Knowledge
CW 97   The Christian Mystery
CW 98   Nature Beings and Spirit Beings – Their Effects in Our Visible
          World
CW 99   The Theosophy of the Rosicrucians
CW 100   Human Development and Christ-Knowledge
CW 101   Myths and Legends. Occult Signs and Symbols
CW 102   The Working into Human Beings by Spiritual Beings
CW 103   The Gospel of John
CW 104   The Apocalypse of John
CW 104a   From the Picture-Script of the Apocalypse of John
CW 105   Universe, Earth, the Human Being: Their Being and
          Development, as well as Their Reflection in the Connection
          between Egyptian Mythology and Modern Culture
CW 106   Egyptian Myths and Mysteries in Relation to the Active Spiritual
          Forces of the Present
CW 107   Spiritual-Scientific Knowledge of the Human Being
CW 108   Answering the Questions of Life and the World through
          Anthroposophy

CW 267   Soul-Exercises: Vol. 1: Exercises with Word and Image
           Meditations for the Methodological Development of Higher
           Powers of Knowledge, 1904-1924
CW 268   Soul-Exercises: Vol. 2: Mantric Verses, 1903-1925
CW 269   Ritual Texts for the Celebration of the Free Christian Religious
           Instruction. The Collected Verses for Teachers and Students of
           the Waldorf School
CW 270   Esoteric Instructions for the First Class of the School for Spiritual
           Science at the Goetheanum 1924, 4 Volumes
CW 271   Art and Knowledge of Art. Foundations of a New Aesthetic
CW 272   Spiritual-Scientific Commentary on Goethe's "Faust" in Two
           Volumes. Vol. 1: Faust, the Striving Human Being
CW 273   Spiritual-Scientific Commentary on Goethe's "Faust" in Two
           Volumes. Vol. 2: The Faust-Problem
CW 274   Addresses for the Christmas Plays from the Old Folk Traditions
CW 275   Art in the Light of Mystery-Wisdom
CW 276   The Artistic in Its Mission in the World. The Genius of
           Language. The World of the Self-Revealing Radiant Appearances
           – Anthroposophy and Art. Anthroposophy and Poetry
CW 277   Eurythmy. The Revelation of the Speaking Soul
CW 277a   The Origin and Development of Eurythmy
CW 278   Eurythmy as Visible Song
CW 279   Eurythmy as Visible Speech
CW 280   The Method and Nature of Speech Formation
CW 281   The Art of Recitation and Declamation
CW 282   Speech Formation and Dramatic Art
CW 283   The Nature of Things Musical and the Experience of Tone in the
           Human Being
CW284/285 Images of Occult Seals and Pillars. The Munich Congress of
           Whitsun 1907 and Its Consequences
CW 286   Paths to a New Style of Architecture. "And the Building Becomes
           Human"
CW 287   The Building at Dornach as a Symbol of Historical Becoming
           and an Artistic Transformation Impulse
CW 288   Style-Forms in the Living Organic
CW 289   The Building-Idea of the Goetheanum: Lectures with Slides from
           the Years 1920-1921
CW 290   The Building-Idea of the Goetheanum: Lectures with Slides from
           the Years 1920-1921
CW 291   The Nature of Colors
CW 291a   Knowledge of Colors. Supplementary Volume to "The Nature of
           Colors"
CW 292   Art History as Image of Inner Spiritual Impulses

SIGNIFICANT EVENTS
IN THE LIFE OF RUDOLF STEINER

1829:   June 23: birth of Johann Steiner (1829-1910)—Rudolf Steiner's father—in Geras, Lower Austria.

1834:   May 8: birth of Franciska Blie (1834-1918)—Rudolf Steiner's mother—in Horn, Lower Austria. "My father and mother were both children of the glorious Lower Austrian forest district north of the Danube."

1860:   May 16: marriage of Johann Steiner and Franciska Blie.

1861:   February 25: birth of *Rudolf Joseph Lorenz Steiner* in Kraljevec, Croatia, near the border with Hungary, where Johann Steiner works as a telegrapher for the South Austria Railroad. Rudolf Steiner is baptized two days later, February 27, the date usually given as his birthday.

1862:   Summer: the family moves to Mödling, Lower Austria.

1863:   The family moves to Pottschach, Lower Austria, near the Styrian border, where Johann Steiner becomes stationmaster. "The view stretched to the mountains...majestic peaks in the distance and the sweet charm of nature in the immediate surroundings."

1864:   November 15: birth of Rudolf Steiner's sister, Leopoldine (d. November 1, 1927). She will become a seamstress and live with her parents for the rest of her life.

1866:   July 28: birth of Rudolf Steiner's deaf-mute brother, Gustav (d. May 1, 1941).

1867:   Rudolf Steiner enters the village school. Following a disagreement between his father and the schoolmaster, whose wife falsely accused the boy of causing a commotion, Rudolf Steiner is taken out of school and taught at home.

1868:   A critical experience. Unknown to the family, an aunt dies in a distant town. Sitting in the station waiting room, Rudolf Steiner sees her "form," which speaks to him, asking for help. "Beginning with this experience, a new soul life began in the boy, one in which not only the outer trees and mountains spoke to him, but also the worlds that lay behind them. From this moment on, the boy began to live with the spirits of nature...."

1869:   The family moves to the peaceful, rural village of Neudorfl, near Wiener-Neustadt in present-day Hungary. Rudolf Steiner attends the village school. Because of the "unorthodoxy" of his writing and spelling, he has to do "extra lessons."

1870:   Through a book lent to him by his tutor, he discovers geometry: "To grasp something purely in the spirit brought me inner happiness. I know that I first learned happiness through geometry." The same tutor allows him to draw, while other students still struggle with their reading and writing. "An artistic element" thus enters his education.

1871:   Though his parents are not religious, Rudolf Steiner becomes a "church child," a favorite of the priest, who was "an exceptional character." "Up to the age of ten or eleven, among those I came to know, he was far and away the most significant." Among other things, he introduces Steiner to Copernican, heliocentric cosmology. As an altar boy, Rudolf Steiner serves at Masses, funerals, and Corpus Christi processions. At year's end, after an incident in which he escapes a thrashing, his father forbids him to go to church.

1872:   Rudolf Steiner transfers to grammar school in Wiener-Neustadt, a five-mile walk from home, which must be done in all weathers.

1873-75: Through his teachers and on his own, Rudolf Steiner has many wonderful experiences with science and mathematics. Outside school, he teaches himself analytic geometry, trigonometry, differential equations, and calculus.

1876:   Rudolf Steiner begins tutoring other students. He learns bookbinding from his father. He also teaches himself stenography.

1877:   Rudolf Steiner discovers Kant's *Critique of Pure Reason*, which he reads and rereads. He also discovers and reads von Rotteck's *World History*.

1878:   He studies extensively in contemporary psychology and philosophy.

1879:   Rudolf Steiner graduates from high school with honors. His father is transferred to Inzersdorf, near Vienna. He uses his first visit to Vienna "to purchase a great number of philosophy books"—Kant, Fichte, Schelling, and Hegel, as well as numerous histories of philosophy. His aim: to find a path from the "I" to nature.

October 1879-1883: Rudolf Steiner attends the Technical College in Vienna—to study mathematics, chemistry, physics, mineralogy, botany, zoology, biology, geology, and mechanics—with a scholarship. He also attends lectures in history and literature, while avidly reading philosophy on his own. His two favorite professors are Karl Julius Schröer (German language and literature) and Edmund Reitlinger (physics). He also audits lectures by Robert Zimmerman on aesthetics and Franz Brentano on philosophy. During this year he begins his friendship with Moritz Zitter (1861-1921), who will help support him financially when he is in Berlin.

1880:   Rudolf Steiner attends lectures on Schiller and Goethe by Karl Julius Schröer, who becomes his mentor. Also "through a remarkable combination of circumstances," he meets Felix Koguzki, an "herb gatherer" and healer, who could "see deeply into the secrets of nature." Rudolf Steiner will meet and study with this "emissary of the Master" throughout his time in Vienna.

1881:   January: "… I didn't sleep a wink. I was busy with philosophical problems until about 12:30 a.m. Then, finally, I threw myself down on my couch. All my striving during the previous year had been to research whether the following statement by Schelling was true or not: *Within everyone dwells a secret, marvelous capacity to draw back from the stream of time—out of the self clothed in all that comes to us from outside—into our innermost being and there, in the immutable form of the Eternal, to look into ourselves.* I believe, and I am still quite certain of it, that I discovered this capacity in myself; I had long had an inkling of it. Now the whole of idealist philosophy stood before me in modified form. What's a sleepless night compared to that!"

Rudolf Steiner begins communicating with leading thinkers of the day, who send him books in return, which he reads eagerly.

July: "I am not one of those who dives into the day like an animal in human form. I pursue a quite specific goal, an idealistic aim—knowledge of the truth! This cannot be done offhandedly. It requires the greatest striving in the world, free of all egotism, and equally of all resignation."

August: Steiner puts down on paper for the first time thoughts for a "Philosophy of Freedom." "The striving for the absolute: this human yearning is freedom." He also seeks to outline a "peasant philosophy," describing what the worldview of a "peasant"—one who lives close to the earth and the old ways—really is.

1881-1882: Felix Koguzki, the herb gatherer, reveals himself to be the envoy of another, higher initiatory personality, who instructs Rudolf Steiner to penetrate Fichte's philosophy and to master modern scientific thinking as a preparation for right entry into the spirit. This "Master" also teaches him the double (evolutionary and involutionary) nature of time.

1882: Through the offices of Karl Julius Schröer, Rudolf Steiner is asked by Joseph Kurschner to edit Goethe's scientific works for the *Deutschen National-Literatur* edition. He writes "A Possible Critique of Atomistic Concepts" and sends it to Friedrich Theodore Vischer.

1883: Rudolf Steiner completes his college studies and begins work on the Goethe project.

1884: First volume of Goethe's *Scientific Writings* (CW 1) appears (March). He lectures on Goethe and Lessing, and Goethe's approach to science. In July, he enters the household of Ladislaus and Pauline Specht as tutor to the four Specht boys. He will live there until 1890. At this time, he meets Josef Breuer (1842-1925), the coauthor with Sigmund Freud of *Studies in Hysteria*, who is the Specht family doctor.

1885: While continuing to edit Goethe's writings, Rudolf Steiner reads deeply in contemporary philosophy (Edouard von Hartmann, Johannes Volkelt, and Richard Wahle, among others).

1886: May: Rudolf Steiner sends Kurschner the manuscript of *Outlines of Goethe's Theory of Knowledge* (CW 2), which appears in October, and which he sends out widely. He also meets the poet Marie Eugenie Delle Grazie and writes "Nature and Our Ideals" for her. He attends her salon, where he meets many priests, theologians, and philosophers, who will become his friends. Meanwhile, the director of the Goethe Archive in Weimar requests his collaboration with the *Sophien* edition of Goethe's works, particularly the writings on color.

1887: At the beginning of the year, Rudolf Steiner is very sick. As the year progresses and his health improves, he becomes increasingly "a man of letters," lecturing, writing essays, and taking part in Austrian cultural life. In August-September, the second volume of Goethe's *Scientific Writings* appears.

1888: January-July: Rudolf Steiner assumes editorship of the "German Weekly" (*Deutsche Wochenschrift*). He begins lecturing more intensively, giving, for example, a lecture titled "Goethe as Father of a New Aesthetics." He meets and becomes soul friends with Friedrich Eckstein (1861-1939), a vegetarian, philosopher of symbolism, alchemist, and musician, who will introduce him to various spiritual currents (including Theosophy) and with whom he will meditate and interpret esoteric and alchemical texts.

1889: Rudolf Steiner first reads Nietzsche (*Beyond Good and Evil*). He encounters Theosophy again and learns of Madame Blavatsky in the Theosophical circle around Marie Lang (1858-1934). Here he also meets well-known figures of Austrian life, as well as esoteric figures like the occultist Franz Hartman and Karl Leinigen-Billigen (translator of C.G. Harrison's *The Transcendental Universe*.) During this period, Steiner first reads A.P. Sinnett's *Esoteric Buddhism* and Mabel Collins's *Light on the Path*. He also begins traveling, visiting Budapest, Weimar, and Berlin (where he meets philosopher Edouard von Hartman).

1890: Rudolf Steiner finishes volume 3 of Goethe's scientific writings. He begins his doctoral dissertation, which will become *Truth and Science* (CW 3). He also meets the poet and feminist Rosa Mayreder (1858-1938), with whom he can exchange his most intimate thoughts. In September, Rudolf Steiner moves to Weimar to work in the Goethe-Schiller Archive.

1891: Volume 3 of the Kurschner edition of Goethe appears. Meanwhile, Rudolf Steiner edits Goethe's studies in mineralogy and scientific writings for the *Sophien* edition. He meets Ludwig Laistner of the Cotta Publishing Company, who asks for a book on the basic question of metaphysics. From this will result, ultimately, *The Philosophy of Freedom* (CW 4), which will be published not by Cotta but by Emil Felber. In October, Rudolf Steiner takes the oral exam for a doctorate in philosophy, mathematics, and mechanics at Rostock University, receiving his doctorate on the twenty-sixth. In November, he gives his first lecture on Goethe's "Fairy Tale" in Vienna.

1892: Rudolf Steiner continues work at the Goethe-Schiller Archive and on his *Philosophy of Freedom*. *Truth and Science*, his doctoral dissertation, is published. Steiner undertakes to write introductions to books on Schopenhauer and Jean Paul for Cotta. At year's end, he finds lodging with Anna Eunike, née Schulz (1853-1911), a widow with four daughters and a son. He also develops a friendship with Otto Erich Hartleben (1864-1905) with whom he shares literary interests.

1893:　Rudolf Steiner begins his habit of producing many reviews and articles. In March, he gives a lecture titled "Hypnotism, with Reference to Spiritism." In September, volume 4 of the Kurschner edition is completed. In November, *The Philosophy of Freedom* appears. This year, too, he meets John Henry Mackay (1864-1933), the anarchist, and Max Stirner, a scholar and biographer.

1894:　Rudolf Steiner meets Elisabeth Förster Nietzsche, the philosopher's sister, and begins to read Nietzsche in earnest, beginning with the as yet unpublished *Antichrist*. He also meets Ernst Haeckel (1834-1919). In the fall, he begins to write *Nietzsche, A Fighter against His Time* (CW 5).

1895:　May, *Nietzsche, A Fighter against His Time* appears.

1896:　January 22: Rudolf Steiner sees Friedrich Nietzsche for the first and only time. Moves between the Nietzsche and the Goethe-Schiller Archives, where he completes his work before year's end. He falls out with Elisabeth Förster Nietzsche, thus ending his association with the Nietzsche Archive.

1897:　Rudolf Steiner finishes the manuscript of *Goethe's Worldview* (CW 6). He moves to Berlin with Anna Eunike and begins editorship of the *Magazin fur Literatur*. From now on, Steiner will write countless reviews, literary and philosophical articles, and so on. He begins lecturing at the "Free Literary Society." In September, he attends the Zionist Congress in Basel. He sides with Dreyfus in the Dreyfus affair.

1898:　Rudolf Steiner is very active as an editor in the political, artistic, and theatrical life of Berlin. He becomes friendly with John Henry Mackay and poet Ludwig Jacobowski (1868-1900). He joins Jacobowski's circle of writers, artists, and scientists—"The Coming Ones" (*Die Kommenden*)—and contributes lectures to the group until 1903. He also lectures at the "League for College Pedagogy." He writes an article for Goethe's sesquicentennial, "Goethe's Secret Revelation," on the "Fairy Tale of the Green Snake and the Beautiful Lily."

1888-89:　"This was a trying time for my soul as I looked at Christianity. . . . I was able to progress only by contemplating, by means of spiritual perception, the evolution of Christianity . . . . Conscious knowledge of real Christianity began to dawn in me around the turn of the century. This seed continued to develop. My soul trial occurred shortly before the beginning of the twentieth century. It was decisive for my soul's development that I stood spiritually before the Mystery of Golgotha in a deep and solemn celebration of knowledge."

1899:　Rudolf Steiner begins teaching and giving lectures and lecture cycles at the Workers' College, founded by Wilhelm Liebknecht (1826-1900). He will continue to do so until 1904. Writes: *Literature and Spiritual Life in the Nineteenth Century; Individualism in Philosophy; Haeckel and His Opponents; Poetry in the Present;* and begins what will become (fifteen years later). *The Riddles of Philosophy* (CW 18). He also meets many artists and writers, including Käthe Kollwitz, Stefan

Zweig, and Rainer Maria Rilke. On October 31, he marries Anna Eunike.

1900: "I thought that the turn of the century must bring humanity a new light. It seemed to me that the separation of human thinking and willing from the spirit had peaked. A turn or reversal of direction in human evolution seemed to me a necessity." Rudolf Steiner finishes *World and Life Views in the Nineteenth Century* (the second part of what will become *The Riddles of Philosophy*) and dedicates it to Ernst Haeckel. It is published in March. He continues lecturing at *Die Kommenden*, whose leadership he assumes after the death of Jacobowski. Also, he gives the Gutenberg Jubilee lecture before 7,000 typesetters and printers. In September, Rudolf Steiner is invited by Count and Countess Brockdorff to lecture in the Theosophical Library. His first lecture is on Nietzsche. His second lecture is titled "Goethe's Secret Revelation." October 6, he begins a lecture cycle on the mystics that will become *Mystics after Modernism* (CW 7). November-December: "Marie von Sivers appears in the audience...." Also in November, Steiner gives his first lecture at the Giordano Bruno Bund (where he will continue to lecture until May, 1905). He speaks on Bruno and modern Rome, focusing on the importance of the philosophy of Thomas Aquinas as monism.

1901: In continual financial straits, Rudolf Steiner's early friends Moritz Zitter and Rosa Mayreder help support him. In October, he begins the lecture cycle *Christianity as Mystical Fact* (CW 8) at the Theosophical Library. In November, he gives his first "Theosophical lecture" on Goethe's "Fairy Tale" in Hamburg at the invitation of Wilhelm Hubbe-Schleiden. He also attends a tea to celebrate the founding of the Theosophical Society at Count and Countess Brockdorff's. He gives a lecture cycle, "From Buddha to Christ," for the circle of the *Kommenden*. November 17, Marie von Sivers asks Rudolf Steiner if Theosophy does not need a Western-Christian spiritual movement (to complement Theosophy's Eastern emphasis). "The question was posed. Now, following spiritual laws, I could begin to give an answer...." In December, Rudolf Steiner writes his first article for a Theosophical publication. At year's end, the Brockdorffs and possibly Wilhelm Hubbe-Schleiden ask Rudolf Steiner to join the Theosophical Society and undertake the leadership of the German section. Rudolf Steiner agrees, on the condition that Marie von Sivers (then in Italy) work with him.

1902: Beginning in January, Rudolf Steiner attends the opening of the Workers' School in Spandau with Rosa Luxemburg (1870-1919). January 17, Rudolf Steiner joins the Theosophical Society. In April, he is asked to become general secretary of the German Section of the Theosophical Society, and works on preparations for its founding. In July, he visits London for a Theosophical congress. He meets Bertram

Keightly, G.R.S. Mead, A.P. Sinnett, and Annie Besant, among others. In September, *Christianity as Mystical Fact* appears. In October, Rudolf Steiner gives his first public lecture on Theosophy ("Monism and Theosophy") to about three hundred people at the Giordano Bruno Bund. On October 19-21, the German Section of the Theosophical Society has its first meeting; Rudolf Steiner is the general secretary, and Annie Besant attends. Steiner lectures on practical karma studies. On October 23, Annie Besant inducts Rudolf Steiner into the Esoteric School of the Theosophical Society. On October 25, Steiner begins a weekly series of lectures: "The Field of Theosophy." During this year, Rudolf Steiner also first meets Ita Wegman (1876-1943), who will become his close collaborator in his final years.

1903:   Rudolf Steiner holds about 300 lectures and seminars. In May, the first issue of the periodical *Luzifer* appears. In June, Rudolf Steiner visits London for the first meeting of the Federation of the European Sections of the Theosophical Society, where he meets Colonel Olcott. He begins to write *Theosophy* (CW 9).

1904:   Rudolf Steiner continues lecturing at the Workers' College and else-where (about 90 lectures), while lecturing intensively all over Germany among Theosophists (about a 140 lectures). In February, he meets Carl Unger (1878-1929), who will become a member of the board of the Anthroposophical Society (1913). In March, he meets Michael Bauer (1871-1929), a Christian mystic, who will also be on the board. In May, *Theosophy* appears, with the dedication: "To the spirit of Giordano Bruno." Rudolf Steiner and Marie von Sivers visit London for meetings with Annie Besant. June: Rudolf Steiner and Marie von Sivers attend the meeting of the Federation of European Sections of the Theosophical Society in Amsterdam. In July, Steiner begins the articles in *Luzifer-Gnosis* that will become *How to Know Higher Worlds* (CW 10) and *Cosmic Memory* (CW 11). In September, Annie Besant visits Germany. In December, Steiner lectures on Freemasonry. He mentions the High Grade Masonry derived from John Yarker and represented by Theodore Reuss and Karl Kellner as a blank slate "into which a good image could be placed."

1905:   This year, Steiner ends his non-Theosophical lecturing activity. Supported by Marie von Sivers, his Theosophical lecturing—both in public and in the Theosophical Society—increases significantly: "The German Theosophical Movement is of exceptional importance." Steiner recommends reading, among others, Fichte, Jacob Boehme, and Angelus Silesius. He begins to introduce Christian themes into Theosophy. He also begins to work with doctors (Felix Peipers and Ludwig Noll). In July, he is in London for the Federation of European Sections, where he attends a lecture by Annie Besant: "I have seldom seen Mrs. Besant speak in so inward and heartfelt a manner...." "Through Mrs. Besant I have found the way to H.P. Blavatsky."

September to October, he gives a course of thirty-one lectures for a small group of esoteric students. In October, the annual meeting of the German Section of the Theosophical Society, which still remains very small, takes place. Rudolf Steiner reports membership has risen from 121 to 377 members. In November, seeking to establish esoteric "continuity," Rudolf Steiner and Marie von Sivers participate in a "Memphis-Misraim" Masonic ceremony. They pay forty-five marks for membership. "Yesterday, you saw how little remains of former esoteric institutions." "We are dealing only with a 'framework'… for the present, nothing lies behind it. The occult powers have completely withdrawn."

1906: Expansion of Theosophical work. Rudolf Steiner gives about 245 lectures, only 44 of which take place in Berlin. Cycles are given in Paris, Leipzig, Stuttgart, and Munich. Esoteric work also intensifies. Rudolf Steiner begins writing *An Outline of Esoteric Science* (CW 13). In January, Rudolf Steiner receives permission (a patent) from the Great Orient of the Scottish A & A Thirty-Three Degree Rite of the Order of the Ancient Freemasons of the Memphis-Misraim Rite to direct a chapter under the name "Mystica Aeterna." This will become the "Cognitive Cultic Section" (also called "Misraim Service") of the Esoteric School. (See: *From the History and Contents of the Cognitive Cultic Section* (CW 264). During this time, Steiner also meets Albert Schweitzer. In May, he is in Paris, where he visits Edouard Schuré. Many Russians attend his lectures (including Konstantin Balmont, Dimitri Mereszkovski, Zinaida Hippius, and Maximilian Woloshin). He attends the General Meeting of the European Federation of the Theosophical Society, at which Col. Olcott is present for the last time. He spends the year's end in Venice and Rome, where he writes and works on his translation of H.P. Blavatsky's *Key to Theosophy*.

1907: Further expansion of the German Theosophical Movement according to the Rosicrucian directive to "introduce spirit into the world"—in education, in social questions, in art, and in science. In February, Col. Olcott dies in Adyar. Before he dies, Olcott indicates that "the Masters" wish Annie Besant to succeed him: much politicking ensues. Rudolf Steiner supports Besant's candidacy. April-May: preparations for the Congress of the Federation of European Sections of the Theosophical Society—the great, watershed Whitsun "Munich Congress," attended by Annie Besant and others. Steiner decides to separate Eastern and Western (Christian-Rosicrucian) esoteric schools. He takes his esoteric school out of the Theosophical Society (Besant and Rudolf Steiner are "in harmony" on this). Steiner makes his first lecture tours to Austria and Hungary. That summer, he is in Italy. In September, he visits Edouard Schuré, who will write the introduction to the French edition of *Christianity as Mystical Fact* in Barr, Alsace. Rudolf Steiner writes the autobiographical statement known as the "Barr Document." In *Luzifer–Gnosis*, "The Education of the Child" appears.

1908:   The movement grows (membership: 1150). Lecturing expands. Steiner makes his first extended lecture tour to Holland and Scandinavia, as well as visits to Naples and Sicily. Themes: St. John's Gospel, the Apocalypse, Egypt, science, philosophy, and logic. *Luzifer-Gnosis* ceases publication. In Berlin, Marie von Sivers (with Johanna Mücke (1864-1949) forms the *Philosophisch-Theosophisch* (after 1915 *Philosophisch-Anthroposophisch*) *Verlag* to publish Steiner's work. Steiner gives lecture cycles titled *The Gospel of St. John* (CW 103) and *The Apocalypse* (104).

1909:   *An Outline of Esoteric Science* appears. Lecturing and travel continues. Rudolf Steiner's spiritual research expands to include the polarity of Lucifer and Ahriman; the work of great individualities in history; the Maitreya Buddha and the Bodhisattvas; spiritual economy (CW 109); the work of the spiritual hierarchies in heaven and on Earth (CW 110). He also deepens and intensifies his research into the Gospels, giving lectures on the Gospel of St. Luke (CW 114) with the first mention of two Jesus children. Meets and becomes friends with Christian Morgenstern (1871-1914). In April, he lays the foundation stone for the Malsch model—the building that will lead to the first Goetheanum. In May, the International Congress of the Federation of European Sections of the Theosophical Society takes place in Budapest. Rudolf Steiner receives the Subba Row medal for *How to Know Higher Worlds*. During this time, Charles W. Leadbeater discovers Jiddu Krishnamurti (1895-1986) and proclaims him the future "world teacher," the bearer of the Maitreya Buddha and the "reappearing Christ." In October, Steiner delivers seminal lectures on "anthroposophy," which he will try, unsuccessfully, to rework over the next years into the unfinished work, *Anthroposophy (A Fragment)* (CW 45).

1910:   New themes: *The Reappearance of Christ in the Etheric* (CW 118); *The Fifth Gospel; The Mission of Folk Souls* (CW 121); *Occult History* (CW 126); the evolving development of etheric cognitive capacities. Rudolf Steiner continues his Gospel research with *The Gospel of St. Matthew* (CW 123). In January, his father dies. In April, he takes a month-long trip to Italy, including Rome, Monte Cassino, and Sicily. He also visits Scandinavia again. July-August, he writes the first mystery drama, *The Portal of Initiation* (CW 14). In November, he gives "psychosophy" lectures. In December, he submits "On the Psychological Foundations and Epistemological Framework of Theosophy" to the International Philosophical Congress in Bologna.

1911:   The crisis in the Theosophical Society deepens. In January, "The Order of the Rising Sun," which will soon become "The Order of the Star in the East," is founded for the coming world teacher, Krishnamurti. At the same time, Marie von Sivers, Rudolf Steiner's coworker, falls ill. Fewer lectures are given, but important new ground is broken. In Prague, in March, Steiner meets Franz Kafka (1883-1924) and Hugo Bergmann (1883-1975). In April, he delivers his paper to the

Philosophical Congress. He writes the second mystery drama, *The Soul's Probation* (CW 14). Also, while Marie von Sivers is convalescing, Rudolf Steiner begins work on *Calendar 1912/1913*, which will contain the "Calendar of the Soul" meditations. On March 19, Anna (Eunike) Steiner dies. In September, Rudolf Steiner visits Einsiedeln, birthplace of Paracelsus. In December, Friedrich Rittelmeyer, future founder of the Christian Community, meets Rudolf Steiner. The *Johannes-Bauverein*, the "building committee," which would lead to the first Goetheanum (first planned for Munich), is also founded, and a preliminary committee for the founding of an independent association is created that, in the following year, will become the Anthroposophical Society. Important lecture cycles include *Occult Physiology* (CW 128); *Wonders of the World* (CW 129); *From Jesus to Christ* (CW 131). Other themes: esoteric Christianity; Christian Rosenkreutz; the spiritual guidance of humanity; the sense world and the world of the spirit.

1912: Despite the ongoing, now increasing crisis in the Theosophical Society, much is accomplished: *Calendar 1912/1913* is published; eurythmy is created; both the third mystery drama, *The Guardian of the Threshold* (CW 14) and *A Way of Self-Knowledge* (CW 16) are written. New (or renewed) themes included life between death and rebirth and karma and reincarnation. Other lecture cycles: *Spiritual Beings in the Heavenly Bodies and the Kingdoms of Nature* (CW 136); *The Human Being in the Light of Occultism, Theosophy, and Philosophy* (CW 137); *The Gospel of St. Mark* (CW 139); and *The Bhagavad Gita and the Epistles of Paul* (CW 142). On May 8, Rudolf Steiner celebrates White Lotus Day, H.P. Blavatsky's death day, which he had faithfully observed for the past decade, for the last time. In August, Rudolf Steiner suggests the "independent association" be called the "Anthroposophical Society." In September, the first eurythmy course takes place. In October, Rudolf Steiner declines recognition of a Theosophical Society lodge dedicated to the Star of the East and decides to expel all Theosophical Society members belonging to the order. Also, with Marie von Sivers, he first visits Dornach, near Basel, Switzerland, and they stand on the hill where the Goetheanum will be. In November, a Theosophical Society lodge is opened by direct mandate from Adyar (Annie Besant). In December, a meeting of the German section occurs at which it is decided that belonging to the Order of the Star of the East is incompatible with membership in the Theosophical Society. December 28: informal founding of the Anthroposophical Society in Berlin.

1913: Expulsion of the German section from the Theosophical Society. February 2-3: Foundation meeting of the Anthroposophical Society. Board members include: Marie von Sivers, Michael Bauer, and Carl Unger. September 20: Laying of the foundation stone for the *Johannes Bau* (Goetheanum) in Dornach. Building begins immediately. The third mystery drama, *The Soul's Awakening* (CW 14), is completed.

Also: *The Threshold of the Spiritual World* (CW 147). Lecture cycles include: *The Bhagavad Gita and the Epistles of Paul* and *The Esoteric Meaning of the Bhagavad Gita* (CW 146), which the Russian philosopher Nikolai Berdyaev attends; *The Mysteries of the East and of Christianity* (CW 144); *The Effects of Esoteric Development* (CW 145); and *The Fifth Gospel* (CW 148). In May, Rudolf Steiner is in London and Paris, where anthroposophical work continues.

1914: Building continues on the *Johannes Bau* (Goetheanum) in Dornach, with artists and coworkers from seventeen nations. The general assembly of the Anthroposophical Society takes place. In May, Rudolf Steiner visits Paris, as well as Chartres Cathedral. June 28: assassination in Sarajevo ("Now the catastrophe has happened!"). August 1: War is declared. Rudolf Steiner returns to Germany from Dornach—he will travel back and forth. He writes the last chapter of *The Riddles of Philosophy*. Lecture cycles include: *Human and Cosmic Thought* (CW 151); *Inner Being of Humanity between Death and a New Birth* (CW 153); *Occult Reading and Occult Hearing* (CW 156). December 24: marriage of Rudolf Steiner and Marie von Sivers.

1915: Building continues. Life after death becomes a major theme, also art. Writes: *Thoughts during a Time of War* (CW 24). Lectures include: *The Secret of Death* (CW 159); *The Uniting of Humanity through the Christ Impulse* (CW 165).

1916: Rudolf Steiner begins work with Edith Maryon (1872-1924) on the sculpture "The Representative of Humanity" ("The Group"—Christ, Lucifer, and Ahriman). He also works with the alchemist Alexander von Bernus on the quarterly *Das Reich*. He writes *The Riddle of Humanity* (CW 20). Lectures include: *Necessity and Freedom in World History and Human Action* (CW 166); *Past and Present in the Human Spirit* (CW 167); *The Karma of Vocation* (CW 172); *The Karma of Untruthfulness* (CW 173).

1917: Russian Revolution. The U.S. enters the war. Building continues. Rudolf Steiner delineates the idea of the "threefold nature of the human being" (in a public lecture March 15) and the "threefold nature of the social organism" (hammered out in May-June with the help of Otto von Lerchenfeld and Ludwig Polzer-Hoditz in the form of two documents titled *Memoranda*, which were distributed in high places). August-September: Rudolf Steiner writes *The Riddles of the Soul* (CW 20). Also: commentary on "The Chemical Wedding of Christian Rosenkreutz" for Alexander Bernus (*Das Reich*). Lectures include: *The Karma of Materialism* (CW 176); *The Spiritual Background of the Outer World: The Fall of the Spirits of Darkness* (CW 177).

1918: March 18: peace treaty of Brest-Litovsk—"Now everything will truly enter chaos! What is needed is cultural renewal." June: Rudolf Steiner visits Karlstein (Grail) Castle outside Prague. Lecture cycle: *From Symptom to Reality in Modern History* (CW 185). In mid-November,

Emil Molt, of the Waldorf-Astoria Cigarette Company, has the idea of founding a school for his workers' children.

1919: Focus on the threefold social organism: tireless travel, countless lectures, meetings, and publications. At the same time, a new public stage of Anthroposophy emerges as cultural renewal begins. The coming years will see initiatives in pedagogy, medicine, pharmacology, and agriculture. January 27: threefold meeting: " We must first of all, with the money we have, found free schools that can bring people what they need." February: first public eurythmy performance in Zurich. Also: "Appeal to the German People" (CW 24), circulated March 6 as a newspaper insert. In April, *Toward Social Renewal* (CW 23)—"perhaps the most widely read of all books on politics appearing since the war"—appears. Rudolf Steiner is asked to undertake the "direction and leadership" of the school founded by the Waldorf-Astoria Company. Rudolf Steiner begins to talk about the "renewal" of education. May 30: a building is selected and purchased for the future Waldorf School. August-September, Rudolf Steiner gives a lecture course for Waldorf teachers, *The Foundations of Human Experience (Study of Man)* (CW 293). September 7: Opening of the first Waldorf School. December (into January): first science course, the *Light Course* (CW 320).

1920: The Waldorf School flourishes. New threefold initiatives. Founding of limited companies *Der Kommenden Tag* and *Futurum A.G.* to infuse spiritual values into the economic realm. Rudolf Steiner also focuses on the sciences. Lectures: *Introducing Anthroposophical Medicine* (CW 312); *The Warmth Course* (CW 321); *The Boundaries of Natural Science* (CW 322); *The Redemption of Thinking* (CW 74). February: Johannes Werner Klein—later a cofounder of the Christian Community—asks Rudolf Steiner about the possibility of a "religious renewal," a "Johannine church." In March, Rudolf Steiner gives the first course for doctors and medical students. In April, a divinity student asks Rudolf Steiner a second time about the possibility of religious renewal. September 27-October 16: anthroposophical "university course." December: lectures titled *The Search for the New Isis* (CW 202).

1921: Rudolf Steiner continues his intensive work on cultural renewal, including the uphill battle for the threefold social order. "University" arts, scientific, theological, and medical courses include: *The Astronomy Course* (CW 323); *Observation, Mathematics, and Scientific Experiment* (CW 324); the *Second Medical Course* (CW 313); *Color*. In June and September-October, Rudolf Steiner also gives the first two "priests' courses" (CW 342 and 343). The "youth movement" gains momentum. Magazines are founded: *Die Drei* (January), and—under the editorship of Albert Steffen (1884-1963)—the weekly, *Das Goetheanum* (August). In February-March, Rudolf Steiner takes his first trip outside Germany since the war (Holland). On April 7, Steiner receives a letter regarding "religious renewal," and May 22-23, he agrees to address the question in a practical way. In June, the Klinical-Therapeutic Institute opens in Arlesheim under the direction of Dr. Ita Wegman. In August, the Chemical-Pharmaceutical Laboratory opens in Arlesheim (Oskar Schmiedel and Ita Wegman, directors). The Clinical Therapeutic Institute is inaugurated in Stuttgart (Dr. Ludwig Noll, director); also the Research Laboratory in Dornach (Ehrenfried Pfeiffer and Gunther Wachsmuth, directors). In November-December, Rudolf Steiner visits Norway.

1922:   The first half of the year involves very active public lecturing (thousands attend); in the second half, Rudolf Steiner begins to withdraw and turn toward the Society—"The Society is asleep." It is "too weak" to do what is asked of it. The businesses—*Die Kommenden Tag* and *Futura A.G.*—fail. In January, with the help of an agent, Steiner undertakes a twelve-city German tour, accompanied by eurythmy performances. In two weeks he speaks to more than 2,000 people. In April, he gives a "university course" in The Hague. He also visits England. In June, he is in Vienna for the East-West Congress. In August-September, he is back in England for the Oxford Conference on Education. Returning to Dornach, he gives the lectures *Philosophy, Cosmology, and Religion* (CW 215), and gives the third priest's course (CW 344). On September 16, The Christian Community is founded. In October-November, Steiner is in Holland and England. He also speaks to the youth: *The Youth Course* (CW 217). In December, Steiner gives lectures titled *The Origins of Natural Science* (CW 326), and *Humanity and the World of Stars: The Spiritual Communion of Humanity* (CW 219). December 31: Fire at the Goetheanum, which is destroyed.

1923:   Despite the fire, Rudolf Steiner continues his work unabated. A very hard year. Internal dispersion, dissension, and apathy abound. There is conflict—between old and new visions—within the society. A wake-up call is needed, and Rudolf Steiner responds with renewed lecturing vitality. His focus: the spiritual context of human life; initiation science; the course of the year; and community building. As a foundation for an artistic school, he creates a series of pastel sketches. Lecture cycles: *The Anthroposophical Movement; Initiation Science* (CW 227) (in England at the Penmaenmawr Summer School); *The Four Seasons and the Archangels* (CW 229); *Harmony of the Creative Word* (CW 230); *The Supersensible Human* (CW 231), given in Holland for the founding of the Dutch society. On November 10, in response to the failed Hitler-Ludendorf putsch in Munich, Steiner closes his Berlin residence and moves the *Philosophisch-Anthroposophisch Verlag* (Press) to Dornach. On December 9, Steiner begins the serialization of his *Autobiography: The Course of My Life* (CW 28) in *Das Goetheanum*. It will continue to appear weekly, without a break, until his death. Late December-early January: Rudolf Steiner refounds the Anthroposophical Society (about 12,000 members internationally) and takes over its leadership. The new board members are: Marie Steiner, Ita Wegman, Albert Steffen, Elizabeth Vreede, and Guenther Wachsmuth. (See *The Christmas Meeting for the Founding of the General Anthroposophical Society* (CW 260). Accompanying lectures: *Mystery Knowledge and Mystery Centers* (CW 232); *World History in the Light of Anthroposophy* (CW 233). December 25: the Foundation Stone is laid (in the hearts of members) in the form of the "Foundation Stone Meditation."

1924: January 1: having founded the Anthroposophical Society and taken over its leadership, Rudolf Steiner has the task of "reforming" it. The process begins with a weekly newssheet ("What's Happening in the Anthroposophical Society") in which Rudolf Steiner's "Letters to Members" and "Anthroposophical Leading Thoughts" appear (CW 26). The next step is the creation of a new esoteric class, the "first class" of the "University of Spiritual Science" (which was to have been followed, had Rudolf Steiner lived longer, by two more advanced classes). Then comes a new language for Anthroposophy—practical, phenomenological, and direct; and Rudolf Steiner creates the model for the second Goetheanum. He begins the series of extensive "karma" lectures (CW 235-40); and finally, responding to needs, he creates two new initiatives: biodynamic agriculture and curative education. After the middle of the year, rumors begin to circulate regarding Steiner's health. Lectures: January-February, *Anthroposophy* (CW 234); February: *Tone Eurythmy* (CW 278); June: *The Agriculture Course* (CW 327); June-July: Speech [?] Eurythmy (CW 279); *Curative Education* (CW 317); August: (England, "Second International Summer School"), *Initiation Consciousness: True and False Paths in Spiritual Investigation* (CW 243); September: *Pastoral Medicine* (CW 318). On September 26, for the first time, Rudolf Steiner cancels a lecture. On September 28, he gives his last lecture. On September 29, he withdraws to his studio in the carpenter's shop; now he is definitively ill. Cared for by Ita Wegman, he continues working, however, and writing the weekly installments of his *Autobiography* and *Letters to the Members/Leading Thoughts* (CW 26).

1925: Rudolf Steiner, while continuing to work, continues to weaken. He finishes *Extending Practical Medicine* (CW 27) with Ita Wegman. On March 30, around ten in the morning, Rudolf Steiner dies.

INDEX